Dance Unleashed

Discover the Secrets to Graceful Movements and Captivating Performances

Gerard Ruiz

loss due to the information herein, either directly or indirectly. Respective authors own all copyrights not held by the publisher. The information herein is offered for informational purposes solely, and is universal as so. The presentation of the information is without contract or any type of guarantee assurance. The trademarks that are used are without any consent, and the publication of the trademark is without permission or backing by the trademark owner. All trademarks and brands within this book are for clarifying purposes only and are the owned by the owners themselves, not affiliated with this document.

Table of Contents

Chapter 1
Introduction to Dance Unleashed

The Essence of Dance

Dance, in its purest form, is an expression of the soul. It transcends the boundaries of language, culture, and time, allowing individuals to communicate through movement. The essence of dance lies in its ability to convey emotions, tell stories, and connect people on a profound level. It is a universal language that speaks to the heart, inviting both dancers and audiences to embark on a journey of discovery and transformation.

At the core of dance is the rhythm that pulses through every beat, guiding the dancer's movements with an invisible thread. This rhythm is not just a sequence of beats; it is the heartbeat of the dance itself. It dictates the tempo, the mood, and the energy of the performance. Whether it's the slow, deliberate steps of a waltz or the frenetic energy of a hip-hop routine, rhythm is the foundation upon which all dance is built. It is the silent partner that leads the dancer through the choreography, ensuring that each movement is in harmony with the music.

Dance is also an exploration of space. The dancer's body becomes a tool for shaping and defining the space around them. Through leaps, turns, and extensions, dancers carve out their own unique paths, creating a visual tapestry that captivates the audience. The use of space is not limited to the physical dimensions of the stage; it extends to the emotional and psychological realms as well. Dancers use their movements to explore the depths of their emotions, pushing the boundaries of what is possible and inviting the audience to join them on this journey.

The essence of dance is deeply rooted in the connection between the dancer and the music. Music serves as the catalyst for movement, inspiring dancers to express themselves in ways that words cannot. It is the driving force that propels the dancer forward, infusing each step with meaning and purpose. The relationship between music and dance is symbiotic; one cannot exist without the other. Together, they create a powerful synergy that elevates the performance to new heights.

Dance is a celebration of the human body and its incredible capabilities. It is a testament to the strength, flexibility, and grace that reside within each of us. Through dance, individuals can push the limits of their physical abilities, discovering new ways to move and express themselves. The body becomes a canvas, and each movement is a brushstroke that contributes to the overall masterpiece. This celebration of the body is not limited to the physical; it extends to the mind and spirit as well. Dance encourages individuals to embrace their unique qualities, fostering a sense of self-awareness and confidence.

The essence of dance is also found in its ability to bring people together. It is a communal experience that transcends individual differences, fostering a sense of unity and belonging. Dance has the power to break down barriers, creating connections between people from diverse backgrounds and cultures. It is a shared experience that allows individuals to come together in celebration, creating a sense of community and camaraderie. Whether it's a group of friends dancing at a party or a professional dance troupe performing on stage, the bonds formed through dance are strong and enduring.

Dance is a form of storytelling, a way to convey narratives and emotions without the need for words. Each movement, gesture, and expression tells a story, inviting the audience to become part of the narrative. Dancers use their bodies to communicate complex emotions and ideas, creating a dialogue between themselves and the audience. This storytelling aspect of dance is what makes it so powerful and compelling. It allows individuals to explore their own stories, as well as the stories of others, fostering empathy and understanding.

The essence of dance is also found in its ability to inspire and uplift. It is a source of joy and liberation, allowing individuals to escape the confines of everyday life and experience a sense of freedom. Dance has the power to transform, to heal, and to empower. It encourages individuals to embrace their creativity and imagination, pushing the boundaries of what is possible. Through dance, individuals can discover new aspects of themselves, unlocking their potential and finding their true voice.

In the world of dance, there are no limits or boundaries. It is a constantly evolving art form that embraces change and innovation. Dancers are encouraged to experiment, to take risks, and to explore new possibilities. This spirit of exploration and creativity is what keeps dance alive and vibrant. It is a dynamic and ever-changing art form that reflects the diversity and complexity of the human experience.

The essence of dance is a celebration of life itself. It is a reminder of the beauty and wonder that exist in the world, a testament to the resilience and strength of the human spirit. Dance is a reflection of our deepest desires, fears, and dreams. It is a mirror that allows us to see ourselves and the world around us in a new light. Through dance, we can connect with our innermost selves, discovering the essence of who we are and what we are capable of.

Why Dance Matters

Dance is a vital thread woven into the fabric of human culture and society. It transcends mere movement, serving as a profound form of expression that resonates deeply with individuals and communities alike. The significance of dance extends beyond the physical realm, touching upon emotional, social, and even spiritual dimensions. It is an art form that has the power to transform lives, foster connections, and inspire change.

At its core, dance is a celebration of life. It is an embodiment of joy, passion, and creativity, allowing individuals to express themselves in ways that words cannot. Through dance, people can convey a wide range of emotions, from happiness and excitement to sorrow and longing. This emotional expression is not only cathartic for the dancer but also for the audience, who can experience and empathize with the emotions being portrayed. Dance has the unique ability to evoke powerful feelings, creating a shared emotional experience that transcends cultural and linguistic barriers.

Dance also plays a crucial role in preserving cultural heritage and identity. Throughout history, dance has been used as a means of storytelling, passing down traditions, and celebrating cultural milestones. Each dance form carries with it a rich history and cultural significance, reflecting the values, beliefs, and customs of the people who practice it. By engaging in dance, individuals can connect with their roots, gaining a deeper understanding of their cultural identity and heritage. This connection fosters a sense of pride and belonging, strengthening the bonds within communities and across generations.

In addition to its cultural significance, dance is a powerful tool for social connection and community building. It brings people together, creating a sense of unity and camaraderie. Whether it's a group of friends dancing at a social gathering or a community coming together for a cultural festival, dance has the ability to break down barriers and foster inclusivity. It encourages collaboration and teamwork, as dancers must work together to create a harmonious performance. This sense of community extends beyond the dance floor, fostering lasting friendships and connections that enrich individuals' lives.

Dance also has a profound impact on physical and mental well-being. It is a form of exercise that promotes physical fitness, improving strength, flexibility, and coordination. The physical benefits of dance are well-documented, with studies showing that regular dance practice can improve cardiovascular health, enhance muscle tone, and increase overall endurance. Beyond the physical benefits, dance also has a positive impact on mental health. It is a form of self-expression that allows individuals to release stress, boost mood, and increase self-confidence. The act of dancing releases endorphins, the body's natural "feel-good" chemicals, which can help alleviate symptoms of anxiety and depression.

Moreover, dance is a powerful educational tool that fosters creativity, critical thinking, and problem-solving skills. It encourages individuals to think outside the box, explore new ideas, and push the boundaries of what is possible. Through dance, individuals can develop a deeper understanding of themselves and the world around them, gaining valuable insights and perspectives. Dance education also promotes discipline, perseverance, and resilience, as dancers must practice and refine their skills to achieve mastery. These qualities are transferable to other areas of life, equipping individuals with the tools they need to succeed in various endeavors.

Dance also serves as a platform for social change and advocacy. Throughout history, dance has been used as a form of protest and activism, giving voice to marginalized communities and raising awareness about important social issues. It is a powerful medium for storytelling and communication, allowing individuals to convey messages and inspire action. Dance can challenge societal norms, question injustices, and promote equality and inclusivity. By engaging in dance, individuals can become agents of change, using their art to make a positive impact on the world.

In the realm of personal growth and self-discovery, dance offers a unique opportunity for individuals to explore their identities and embrace their authentic selves. It encourages self-reflection and introspection, allowing individuals to connect with their innermost thoughts and feelings. Through dance, individuals can discover new aspects of themselves, unlocking their potential and finding their true voice. This journey of self-discovery is empowering, fostering a sense of confidence and self-assurance that extends beyond the dance floor.

Dance is also an essential component of the performing arts, contributing to the richness and diversity of artistic expression. It is a dynamic and ever-evolving art form that embraces innovation and creativity. Dancers and choreographers are constantly pushing the boundaries of what is possible, exploring new styles, techniques, and concepts. This spirit of exploration and experimentation keeps dance alive and vibrant, ensuring its continued relevance and impact in the world of art and culture.

In the educational context, dance can play a transformative role in shaping young minds and fostering a love for the arts. It provides students with a creative outlet, allowing them to express themselves and explore their interests. Dance education promotes holistic development, nurturing not only physical skills but also cognitive, emotional, and social growth. It encourages students to think critically, collaborate with others, and develop a sense of empathy and understanding. By incorporating dance into the curriculum, educators can create a more engaging and inclusive learning environment that supports the diverse needs and talents of students.

Setting Your Dance Goals

Setting dance goals is an essential step in any dancer's journey, whether you're a beginner just starting out or an experienced performer looking to refine your skills. Goals provide direction and motivation, helping you focus your efforts and measure your progress. They serve as a roadmap, guiding you through the challenges and triumphs of your dance journey. By setting clear and achievable goals, you can unlock your potential and reach new heights in your dance practice.

The first step in setting dance goals is to reflect on your motivations and aspirations. Consider why you are drawn to dance and what you hope to achieve through your practice. Are you looking to improve your technique, explore new dance styles, or perform on stage? Perhaps you want to use dance as a form of self-expression or as a way to connect with others. Understanding your motivations will help you set meaningful goals that align with your values and passions.

Once you have a clear understanding of your motivations, it's time to set specific and measurable goals. Vague goals like "become a better dancer" are difficult to achieve because they lack clarity and direction. Instead, focus on setting goals that are specific and measurable, such as "master the basic steps of salsa" or "perform in a local dance showcase." These goals provide a clear target to aim for and allow you to track your progress over time.

It's also important to set both short-term and long-term goals. Short-term goals are smaller, more immediate objectives that can be achieved in a relatively short period of time, such as a few weeks or months. These goals help build momentum and provide a sense of accomplishment as you work towards your larger aspirations. Long-term goals, on the other hand, are more ambitious objectives that may take several months or even years to achieve. They provide a sense of purpose and direction, guiding your overall dance journey.

As you set your goals, be sure to consider your current skill level and experience. It's important to set goals that are challenging yet achievable, pushing you to grow and improve without becoming overwhelming. If you're a beginner, focus on mastering the fundamentals and building a strong foundation. As you gain experience and confidence, you can set more advanced goals that challenge you to explore new styles and techniques.

In addition to setting specific goals, it's important to create a plan of action to achieve them. Break down your goals into smaller, manageable steps, and create a timeline for completing each step. For example, if your goal is to perform in a local dance showcase, your action plan might include attending regular dance classes, practicing at home, and seeking feedback from instructors or peers. By creating a plan of action, you can stay organized and focused, ensuring that you make steady progress towards your goals.

As you work towards your goals, it's important to stay flexible and open to change. Dance is a dynamic and ever-evolving art form, and your goals may shift as you gain new experiences and insights. Be willing to reassess and adjust your goals as needed, taking into account any new opportunities or challenges that arise. This flexibility will allow you to stay motivated and engaged, ensuring that your goals remain relevant and meaningful.

It's also important to celebrate your achievements along the way. Recognize and acknowledge the progress you've made, no matter how small. Celebrating your successes will boost your confidence and motivation, encouraging you to continue working towards your goals. Whether it's mastering a new dance move or performing in front of an audience, take the time to appreciate your accomplishments and reflect on how far you've come.

In addition to setting individual goals, consider setting goals that involve collaboration and connection with others. Dance is a social art form, and working with others can enhance your learning and growth. Consider joining a dance group or ensemble, participating in workshops or masterclasses, or collaborating with other dancers on a performance project. These collaborative goals can provide new perspectives and insights, enriching your dance journey and fostering a sense of community and camaraderie.

As you set and work towards your dance goals, remember to prioritize self-care and well-being.

Dance can be physically and mentally demanding, and it's important to take care of your body and mind. Make time for rest and recovery, and listen to your body's needs. Incorporate practices such as stretching, meditation, or yoga into your routine to support your overall well-being. By prioritizing self-care, you can ensure that you have the energy and resilience to pursue your goals with passion and dedication.

Finally, remember that the journey is just as important as the destination. While achieving your goals is a rewarding experience, the process of working towards them is where true growth and transformation occur. Embrace the challenges and setbacks as opportunities for learning and development, and savor the moments of joy and discovery along the way. By focusing on the journey, you can cultivate a deeper appreciation for the art of dance and the unique path you are on.

Overcoming Common Dance Myths

Dance, an art form as old as humanity itself, is often shrouded in myths and misconceptions that can deter potential dancers from pursuing their passion. These myths, perpetuated over time, can create unnecessary barriers and foster self-doubt. By debunking these myths, we can open the door to a more inclusive and accessible dance community, where everyone feels welcome to explore the joy of movement.

One of the most pervasive myths is the belief that dance is only for the young. This misconception suggests that if you haven't started dancing by a certain age, it's too late to begin. In reality, dance is for everyone, regardless of age. Many people discover their love for dance later in life, finding it to be a fulfilling and enriching experience. Dance classes are available for all age groups, from toddlers to seniors, and each stage of life brings its own unique perspective and style to the dance floor. The key is to find a class or style that resonates with you and to embrace the journey of learning and growth.

Another common myth is that you need to have a certain body type to be a dancer. This stereotype often portrays dancers as having long, lean bodies, which can discourage those who don't fit this mold from pursuing dance. However, dance is a celebration of diversity and individuality. Every body is a dance body, and each person brings their own unique strengths and qualities to the art form. Dance is about expressing yourself and connecting with others, not about fitting into a specific physical ideal. Embracing your body and its capabilities is an essential part of the dance journey, and many dance communities actively celebrate and promote body positivity and inclusivity.

The notion that dance is only for those with natural talent is another myth that can hinder aspiring dancers. While some individuals may have a natural affinity for movement, dance is a skill that can be developed and refined through practice and dedication. Like any other art form, dance requires time, effort, and perseverance to master. Even the most accomplished dancers have spent countless hours honing their craft, learning new techniques, and pushing their boundaries. The journey of dance is one of continuous learning and growth, and anyone with the passion and commitment to improve can become a skilled dancer.

A related myth is the idea that dance is only for those who want to pursue it professionally. This misconception can discourage individuals who simply want to dance for fun or as a hobby. Dance is a versatile art form that can be enjoyed at any level, whether you're dancing in a professional company, taking classes at a local studio, or simply moving to music in your living room. The joy of dance lies in the experience itself, not in achieving a specific level of proficiency or recognition. Dance can be a source of joy, relaxation, and self-expression, regardless of your goals or aspirations.

The belief that dance is only for women is another stereotype that persists in some circles. While certain dance styles may have historically been associated with one gender, dance is a universal art form that transcends gender boundaries. Men and women alike can find fulfillment and expression through dance, and many dance styles actively encourage participation from all genders. From ballet to hip-hop, contemporary to ballroom, dance offers a wide range of styles and opportunities for everyone to explore and enjoy.

The myth that dance is not a "real" form of exercise is another misconception that deserves to be addressed. Dance is a highly physical activity that offers numerous health benefits, including improved cardiovascular fitness, increased strength and flexibility, and enhanced coordination and balance. It is a full-body workout that engages multiple muscle groups and can burn a significant number of calories. In addition to its physical benefits, dance also promotes mental well-being by reducing stress, boosting mood, and increasing self-confidence. Dance is a holistic form of exercise that nurtures both the body and mind.

Another common myth is that dance is too expensive or inaccessible for most people. While some dance classes or programs may have higher costs, there are many affordable and accessible options available. Community centers, local dance studios, and online platforms often offer classes at a range of price points, making dance accessible to individuals with different budgets. Additionally, many dance communities offer scholarships, sliding scale fees, or volunteer opportunities to help make dance more inclusive and accessible. With a little research and creativity, anyone can find a way to incorporate dance into their life.

The idea that dance is only for those who are outgoing or extroverted is another misconception that can deter individuals from trying dance. Dance is a form of self-expression that can be enjoyed by people of all personality types. Introverts and extroverts alike can find fulfillment and joy in dance, as it provides an opportunity to connect with oneself and others in a meaningful way. Dance can be a powerful tool for self-discovery and personal growth, allowing individuals to explore their emotions and express themselves in a safe and supportive environment.

Finally, the myth that dance is only for those who are coordinated or graceful can be a significant barrier for beginners. While coordination and grace are skills that can enhance a dancer's performance, they are not prerequisites for enjoying dance. Dance is a journey of exploration and learning, and everyone starts somewhere. With practice and perseverance, individuals can develop their coordination, balance, and grace over time. The key is to approach dance with an open mind and a willingness to learn, embracing the process of growth and improvement.

Embracing Your Unique Dance Journey

Every dancer embarks on a unique journey, a path that is as individual as the person taking it. Embracing this journey means acknowledging and celebrating the distinct qualities that make your dance experience truly your own. It involves understanding that your path will be different from others, shaped by your personal experiences, aspirations, and challenges. By embracing your unique dance journey, you can cultivate a deeper connection to the art form and discover the joy and fulfillment that dance can bring.

The first step in embracing your dance journey is to recognize that there is no one-size-fits-all approach to dance. Each dancer brings their own set of strengths, weaknesses, and perspectives to the dance floor. Your journey will be influenced by a variety of factors, including your background, interests, and goals. It's important to honor these differences and resist the temptation to compare yourself to others.

Instead, focus on your own progress and growth, celebrating the milestones and achievements that are meaningful to you.

As you navigate your dance journey, it's essential to cultivate a mindset of openness and curiosity. Dance is a dynamic and ever-evolving art form, and there is always something new to learn and explore. Embrace the opportunity to try different styles, techniques, and approaches, even if they are outside of your comfort zone. This willingness to experiment and take risks can lead to new discoveries and insights, enriching your dance experience and helping you grow as a dancer.

Another important aspect of embracing your dance journey is to develop a strong sense of self-awareness. Take the time to reflect on your motivations, goals, and values as a dancer. What draws you to dance, and what do you hope to achieve through your practice? By gaining a deeper understanding of yourself and your aspirations, you can make more informed decisions about your dance journey and ensure that it aligns with your personal values and passions.

As you progress on your dance journey, it's important to set realistic and achievable goals that reflect your unique path. These goals should be specific and measurable, providing a clear target to aim for and allowing you to track your progress over time. Consider setting both short-term and long-term goals, as well as goals that challenge you to grow and improve. By setting goals that are meaningful to you, you can stay motivated and focused, ensuring that your dance journey remains fulfilling and rewarding.

Embracing your unique dance journey also means being open to feedback and learning from others. Dance is a collaborative art form, and there is much to be gained from the insights and perspectives of fellow dancers, instructors, and mentors. Seek out opportunities to receive constructive feedback and use it as a tool for growth and improvement. At the same time, trust your instincts and intuition, and remember that you are the ultimate authority on your own dance journey.

It's also important to cultivate a sense of resilience and perseverance as you navigate the ups and downs of your dance journey. Dance can be challenging, and there will inevitably be moments of frustration, self-doubt, and setbacks. Embrace these challenges as opportunities for growth and learning, and remember that they are a natural part of the dance journey. By developing resilience and perseverance, you can overcome obstacles and continue to move forward with confidence and determination.

As you embrace your unique dance journey, remember to prioritize self-care and well-being.

Dance is a physically and mentally demanding art form, and it's important to take care of your body and mind. Make time for rest and recovery, and listen to your body's needs. Incorporate practices such as stretching, meditation, or yoga into your routine to support your overall well-being. By prioritizing self-care, you can ensure that you have the energy and resilience to pursue your dance journey with passion and dedication.

Another key aspect of embracing your dance journey is to find joy and fulfillment in the process itself. While achieving your goals is important, the true value of dance lies in the experience of dancing. Embrace the moments of joy, discovery, and connection that dance brings, and savor the journey of growth and transformation. By focusing on the present moment and finding joy in the process, you can cultivate a deeper appreciation for the art of dance and the unique path you are on.

Chapter 2

The Foundations of Graceful Movement

Understanding Body Alignment

Body alignment is a fundamental concept in dance, serving as the foundation for movement, balance, and expression. It refers to the way the body is positioned and organized in space, ensuring that each part is in the correct place relative to the others. Proper alignment not only enhances the aesthetic quality of dance but also promotes efficiency, reduces the risk of injury, and allows for greater freedom of movement. Understanding and mastering body alignment is essential for dancers of all levels, as it lays the groundwork for technical proficiency and artistic expression.

At the heart of body alignment is the concept of the body's center, often referred to as the "core." This area, which includes the muscles of the abdomen, lower back, and pelvis, plays a crucial role in maintaining stability and control. A strong and engaged core provides the support needed to execute movements with precision and grace. It acts as a central axis around which the rest of the body can move, allowing for fluid transitions and dynamic expression. Developing core strength and awareness is a key component of achieving proper alignment and should be a focus of any dancer's training regimen.

In addition to the core, body alignment involves the positioning of the head, shoulders, spine, hips, knees, and feet. Each of these elements must be in harmony with the others to create a balanced and cohesive whole. The head should be aligned with the spine, with the chin slightly tucked and the gaze directed forward. The shoulders should be relaxed and level, allowing for a broad and open chest. The spine should maintain its natural curves, with the pelvis in a neutral position. The hips should be level and aligned with the knees, which should be slightly bent and positioned over the feet. The feet should be parallel and firmly planted on the ground, providing a stable base for movement.

Achieving proper body alignment requires a combination of strength, flexibility, and awareness. Strength is needed to maintain the correct positioning of the body, while flexibility allows for a full range of motion. Awareness, or proprioception, is the ability to sense the position and movement of the body in space. This awareness is developed through practice and repetition, allowing dancers to make subtle adjustments to their alignment as needed. By cultivating these qualities, dancers can achieve a sense of balance and control that enhances their performance and reduces the risk of injury.

One of the most effective ways to develop body alignment is through targeted exercises and conditioning. Pilates, yoga, and other forms of body conditioning can help build core strength, improve flexibility, and increase body awareness. These practices often emphasize alignment and posture, providing valuable tools for dancers to incorporate into their training. Additionally, regular stretching and strengthening exercises can help maintain the flexibility and strength needed for proper alignment.

In the dance studio, mirrors can be a valuable tool for assessing and improving body alignment. By observing their reflection, dancers can gain a visual understanding of their alignment and make necessary adjustments. However, it's important to use mirrors mindfully, as over-reliance on visual feedback can detract from the development of proprioceptive awareness. Dancers should also seek feedback from instructors and peers, who can provide valuable insights and corrections to help refine alignment.

Breath is another important aspect of body alignment, as it influences posture and movement. Proper breathing techniques can help release tension, improve focus, and enhance the flow of movement. Dancers should practice deep, diaphragmatic breathing, allowing the breath to support and guide their movements. By coordinating breath with movement, dancers can achieve a sense of ease and fluidity that enhances their alignment and overall performance.

In addition to physical practice, mental focus and concentration are essential for achieving and maintaining body alignment. Dancers must cultivate a strong mind-body connection, allowing them to remain present and aware of their alignment throughout their practice. Visualization techniques can be helpful in this regard, as they allow dancers to mentally rehearse and reinforce correct alignment. By visualizing the desired alignment and movement, dancers can create a mental blueprint that guides their physical practice.

It's important to recognize that body alignment is not a static concept but a dynamic process that evolves with each movement. As dancers transition from one position to another, they must continuously adjust and refine their alignment to maintain balance and control. This requires a high level of awareness and adaptability, as well as a willingness to experiment and explore different possibilities. By embracing the dynamic nature of alignment, dancers can achieve a greater sense of freedom and expression in their movement.

In the context of performance, body alignment plays a crucial role in conveying emotion and intention. Proper alignment allows dancers to project confidence and presence, enhancing their ability to connect with the audience. It also enables dancers to execute movements with clarity and precision, ensuring that their artistic vision is communicated effectively. By mastering body alignment, dancers can elevate their performance and create a more impactful and memorable experience for their audience.

The Importance of Balance and Control

Balance and control are the twin pillars upon which the art of dance is built. They are the invisible threads that weave through every movement, ensuring fluidity, precision, and grace. Without them, even the most technically proficient dancer can falter. Understanding and mastering these elements is crucial for anyone looking to excel in dance, as they form the foundation for both technical execution and artistic expression.

Balance in dance is the ability to maintain a stable and centered position, whether stationary or in motion. It is the equilibrium that allows dancers to execute complex movements with confidence and poise. Achieving balance requires a keen awareness of the body's alignment and the distribution of weight. It involves engaging the core muscles to support the spine and maintain a neutral pelvis, while also ensuring that the head, shoulders, and limbs are aligned. This alignment creates a stable base from which dancers can move with ease and control.

Control, on the other hand, is the ability to direct and manage movement with precision and intention. It is the mastery over one's body that allows dancers to execute movements with clarity and purpose. Control involves the coordination of muscles and joints to achieve the desired movement, as well as the ability to modulate speed, force, and direction. It requires a deep understanding of the body's mechanics and the ability to make subtle adjustments in response to changes in balance and momentum.

The relationship between balance and control is symbiotic, with each element reinforcing and enhancing the other. Balance provides the stability needed for controlled movement, while control allows dancers to maintain balance even in dynamic and challenging situations. Together, they enable dancers to execute movements with confidence and artistry, creating a seamless and captivating performance.

Developing balance and control requires dedicated practice and training. One effective way to enhance these skills is through exercises that challenge and improve proprioception, or the body's ability to sense its position and movement in space. Activities such as standing on one leg, practicing turns, and performing movements on an unstable surface can help improve proprioceptive awareness and enhance balance. Additionally, exercises that focus on core strength and stability, such as Pilates and yoga, can provide the support needed for maintaining balance and control.

Another important aspect of developing balance and control is understanding the role of breath in movement. Proper breathing techniques can help release tension, improve focus, and enhance the flow of movement. By coordinating breath with movement, dancers can achieve a sense of ease and fluidity that enhances their balance and control. Practicing deep, diaphragmatic breathing can also help calm the mind and reduce anxiety, allowing dancers to remain focused and centered during their practice.

In the dance studio, mirrors can be a valuable tool for assessing and improving balance and control. By observing their reflection, dancers can gain a visual understanding of their alignment and make necessary adjustments. However, it's important to use mirrors mindfully, as over-reliance on visual feedback can detract from the development of proprioceptive awareness. Dancers should also seek feedback from instructors and peers, who can provide valuable insights and corrections to help refine balance and control.

In addition to physical practice, mental focus and concentration are essential for achieving and maintaining balance and control. Dancers must cultivate a strong mind-body connection, allowing them to remain present and aware of their movements throughout their practice. Visualization techniques can be helpful in this regard, as they allow dancers to mentally rehearse and reinforce correct alignment and movement. By visualizing the desired balance and control, dancers can create a mental blueprint that guides their physical practice.

The importance of balance and control extends beyond the technical aspects of dance, influencing the artistic and expressive qualities of performance. Proper balance and control allow dancers to convey emotion and intention with clarity and impact. They enable dancers to execute movements with precision and nuance, ensuring that their artistic vision is communicated effectively. By mastering balance and control, dancers can elevate their performance and create a more impactful and memorable experience for their audience.

In the context of performance, balance and control also play a crucial role in preventing injury. Dance is a physically demanding art form, and the risk of injury is always present. By maintaining proper balance and control, dancers can reduce the strain on their muscles and joints, minimizing the risk of injury. This is particularly important when executing complex or challenging movements, where the potential for injury is higher. By prioritizing balance and control in their practice, dancers can ensure their long-term health and well-being.

Developing Flexibility and Strength

Flexibility and strength are the dynamic duo that empowers dancers to perform with grace, power, and fluidity. These two elements are not only essential for executing movements with precision but also for preventing injuries and enhancing overall performance. Developing flexibility and strength is a continuous journey that requires dedication, consistency, and a well-rounded approach to training.

Flexibility refers to the range of motion available at a joint or group of joints. It allows dancers to achieve the lines, extensions, and fluidity that are characteristic of many dance styles. Flexibility is not just about being able to perform impressive splits or high kicks; it's about having the freedom to move with ease and expressiveness. To develop flexibility, dancers must engage in regular stretching routines that target all major muscle groups. This includes dynamic stretching, which involves moving parts of the body through a full range of motion, and static stretching, where a stretch is held for a period of time to lengthen the muscles.

Dynamic stretching is particularly beneficial as a warm-up before dance practice or performance. It prepares the muscles and joints for movement, increases blood flow, and reduces the risk of injury. Examples of dynamic stretches include leg swings, arm circles, and gentle lunges. These movements should be performed in a controlled manner, gradually increasing in intensity to ensure the body is adequately prepared for the demands of dance.

Static stretching, on the other hand, is best performed after dance practice or as part of a cool-down routine. Holding stretches for 20 to 30 seconds allows the muscles to relax and lengthen, improving flexibility over time. Key areas to focus on include the hamstrings, quadriceps, hip flexors, calves, shoulders, and back. It's important to listen to your body and avoid pushing beyond your limits, as overstretching can lead to injury.

In addition to stretching, incorporating practices such as yoga or Pilates can enhance flexibility while also promoting strength and body awareness. These disciplines emphasize alignment, breath control, and mindful movement, providing a holistic approach to flexibility training. They also offer a variety of poses and exercises that target different muscle groups, helping to create a balanced and flexible body.

Strength, the counterpart to flexibility, is the ability of a muscle or group of muscles to exert force. It provides the power and control needed to execute movements with precision and stability. Developing strength is crucial for dancers, as it supports proper alignment, enhances balance, and allows for dynamic and explosive movements. Strength training should focus on building both muscular endurance and power, targeting all major muscle groups to create a well-rounded and resilient body.

Core strength is particularly important for dancers, as it provides the foundation for stability and control. A strong core supports the spine, aids in balance, and allows for efficient transfer of energy throughout the body. Core exercises such as planks, Russian twists, and leg raises can help build the strength needed for dance. It's important to engage the core during all movements, maintaining a sense of connection and support throughout the body.

In addition to core work, dancers should incorporate exercises that target the legs, arms, and back. Squats, lunges, and calf raises are effective for building lower body strength, while push-ups, tricep dips, and rows can enhance upper body strength. Resistance training, using bands or weights, can also be beneficial for increasing muscle strength and endurance. It's important to maintain proper form and alignment during all exercises to prevent injury and ensure maximum benefit.

Cross-training, or engaging in activities outside of dance, can also be an effective way to develop strength and flexibility. Activities such as swimming, cycling, or martial arts can provide a different stimulus for the muscles, promoting overall fitness and preventing overuse injuries. Cross-training can also enhance cardiovascular endurance, which is important for sustaining energy and performance during dance.

Recovery is a crucial component of developing flexibility and strength. Adequate rest and recovery allow the muscles to repair and grow stronger, reducing the risk of injury and burnout. Dancers should prioritize sleep, hydration, and nutrition to support their training and overall well-being. Incorporating rest days and active recovery, such as gentle stretching or low-intensity activities, can help maintain balance and prevent overtraining.

Listening to your body is essential in the journey of developing flexibility and strength. Each dancer's body is unique, and progress may vary from person to person. It's important to be patient and consistent, celebrating small victories along the way. Setting realistic goals and tracking progress can provide motivation and a sense of accomplishment.

Breathing Techniques for Dancers

Breathing is an often overlooked yet vital component of dance, serving as the bridge between movement and expression. It is the rhythm that underlies every step, turn, and leap, providing dancers with the energy and focus needed to perform at their best. Mastering breathing techniques can enhance a dancer's performance, improve endurance, and reduce the risk of injury. Understanding how to harness the power of breath is essential for dancers of all levels, as it can transform the way they move and connect with their audience.

Breathing is a natural and automatic process, but in the context of dance, it requires conscious attention and control. The breath can influence a dancer's posture, alignment, and overall sense of balance. Proper breathing techniques can help release tension, improve focus, and enhance the flow of movement. By coordinating breath with movement, dancers can achieve a sense of ease and fluidity that elevates their performance.

One of the most fundamental breathing techniques for dancers is diaphragmatic breathing, also known as belly breathing. This technique involves breathing deeply into the diaphragm, allowing the abdomen to expand and contract with each breath. Diaphragmatic breathing promotes relaxation and reduces tension in the upper body, allowing for greater freedom of movement. To practice this technique, dancers should place one hand on their abdomen and the other on their chest, focusing on expanding the abdomen with each inhale and gently contracting it with each exhale. This practice can be incorporated into warm-ups, cool-downs, and moments of rest during dance practice.

In addition to diaphragmatic breathing, dancers can benefit from learning how to synchronize their breath with movement. This technique, often referred to as breath phrasing, involves coordinating inhalations and exhalations with specific movements or sequences. For example, dancers may inhale during a preparatory movement and exhale during an execution or release. Breath phrasing can enhance the dynamics and expression of movement, allowing dancers to convey emotion and intention with greater clarity. Practicing breath phrasing requires awareness and experimentation, as dancers explore different ways to integrate breath into their movement.

Breath control is another important aspect of breathing techniques for dancers. It involves the ability to regulate the depth, speed, and rhythm of breath to support different types of movement. For instance, slow and deep breaths can promote relaxation and focus during sustained movements, while quick and shallow breaths can provide bursts of energy for dynamic and explosive movements. Developing breath control requires practice and mindfulness, as dancers learn to adapt their breathing to the demands of their choreography.

In addition to enhancing performance, proper breathing techniques can also improve a dancer's endurance and stamina. Dance is a physically demanding art form that requires sustained energy and focus. By optimizing their breathing, dancers can increase their oxygen intake and improve their cardiovascular efficiency, allowing them to perform for longer periods without fatigue. Interval training, which involves alternating between periods of high-intensity movement and rest, can be an effective way to improve breath control and endurance. During rest periods, dancers should focus on deep and controlled breathing to recover and prepare for the next interval.

Breathing techniques can also play a crucial role in injury prevention and recovery. Proper breathing can help reduce tension and stress in the body, minimizing the risk of strain and overuse injuries. In the event of an injury, breathing techniques can aid in relaxation and pain management, promoting healing and recovery. Dancers should incorporate breathing exercises into their regular practice to support their overall health and well-being.

In the context of performance, breathing techniques can enhance a dancer's connection with the audience. Breath is a powerful tool for conveying emotion and intention, allowing dancers to communicate their artistic vision with authenticity and impact. By mastering their breath, dancers can create a more immersive and engaging experience for their audience, drawing them into the world of the performance.

To develop effective breathing techniques, dancers should prioritize regular practice and mindfulness. Breathing exercises can be incorporated into daily routines, warm-ups, and cool-downs, allowing dancers to build awareness and control over their breath. Mindfulness practices, such as meditation or yoga, can also support the development of breath awareness and relaxation. By cultivating a strong mind-body connection, dancers can harness the power of breath to enhance their performance and artistic expression.

Building a Strong Dance Foundation

A strong dance foundation is the cornerstone of any dancer's journey, providing the essential skills and techniques needed to excel in the art form. It is the bedrock upon which all other elements of dance are built, from complex choreography to expressive performance. Establishing a solid foundation requires dedication, patience, and a commitment to mastering the basics. For beginners, this journey begins with understanding the fundamental principles of dance and developing the physical and mental attributes necessary for success.

At the heart of a strong dance foundation is the mastery of basic techniques. These techniques serve as the building blocks for more advanced movements and are essential for achieving precision, control, and fluidity. Key elements include posture, alignment, balance, and coordination. Proper posture involves maintaining an upright and aligned position, with the head, shoulders, and hips in line. This alignment provides the stability needed for movement and helps prevent injury. Balance is the ability to maintain a stable position, whether stationary or in motion, and is crucial for executing turns, jumps, and other dynamic movements. Coordination involves the ability to synchronize different parts of the body, allowing for smooth and efficient movement.

To develop these fundamental skills, beginners should focus on regular practice and repetition. Consistent training helps reinforce muscle memory and build the strength and flexibility needed for dance. It's important to start with simple exercises and gradually progress to more complex movements as proficiency improves. This approach allows dancers to build confidence and avoid frustration, ensuring a positive and rewarding experience.

In addition to physical skills, a strong dance foundation requires mental focus and discipline. Dance is as much a mental challenge as it is a physical one, and developing concentration and perseverance is essential for success. Dancers must cultivate the ability to focus on their movements, blocking out distractions and maintaining a clear mind. This mental discipline allows dancers to remain present and engaged during practice and performance, enhancing their ability to learn and grow.

Another important aspect of building a strong dance foundation is understanding musicality and rhythm.

Dance is inherently connected to music, and the ability to interpret and respond to musical cues is a key component of performance. Beginners should practice listening to different types of music, paying attention to tempo, dynamics, and phrasing. This practice helps develop an intuitive sense of timing and rhythm, allowing dancers to move in harmony with the music.

Flexibility and strength are also crucial components of a strong dance foundation. Flexibility allows dancers to achieve the lines and extensions characteristic of many dance styles, while strength provides the power and control needed for movement. Beginners should incorporate regular stretching and strengthening exercises into their training regimen, focusing on all major muscle groups. This balanced approach helps prevent injury and ensures that the body is prepared for the demands of dance.

In the dance studio, feedback from instructors and peers is invaluable for building a strong foundation. Constructive criticism provides insights into areas for improvement and helps dancers refine their technique. It's important to approach feedback with an open mind and a willingness to learn, using it as a tool for growth and development. Dancers should also seek opportunities to observe and learn from more experienced dancers, gaining inspiration and insights from their practice.

Cross-training, or engaging in activities outside of dance, can also support the development of a strong foundation. Activities such as yoga, Pilates, or swimming can enhance flexibility, strength, and cardiovascular endurance, providing a well-rounded approach to fitness. Cross-training can also prevent overuse injuries and promote overall health and well-being.

As beginners progress in their training, setting realistic and achievable goals can provide motivation and a sense of accomplishment. Goals should be specific and measurable, allowing dancers to track their progress and celebrate milestones along the way. It's important to remain patient and persistent, recognizing that building a strong foundation is a gradual process that requires time and effort.

Chapter 3

Mastering Dance Techniques

Exploring Different Dance Styles

Dance is a universal language that transcends cultural and geographical boundaries, offering a rich tapestry of styles and expressions. Each dance style carries its own unique history, technique, and cultural significance, providing dancers with a diverse array of opportunities to explore and express themselves. For beginners, delving into different dance styles can be an exciting and rewarding journey, offering new perspectives and insights into the art form.

Ballet, often considered the foundation of many dance styles, is renowned for its grace, precision, and discipline. Originating in the Italian Renaissance courts and later developed in France and Russia, ballet emphasizes formalized movements and positions, such as pliés, tendus, and arabesques. It requires a strong foundation in technique, including posture, alignment, and turnout. Ballet is characterized by its ethereal quality, with dancers appearing to float effortlessly across the stage. For beginners, ballet provides an excellent introduction to the fundamentals of dance, offering a solid base for exploring other styles.

Contemporary dance, a more modern and expressive form, emerged in the mid-20th century as a reaction against the rigid structure of classical ballet. It incorporates elements of ballet, modern dance, and jazz, allowing for greater freedom and creativity. Contemporary dance often explores abstract concepts and emotions, with an emphasis on fluidity, improvisation, and floor work. It encourages dancers to connect with their inner selves and express their individuality through movement. For those seeking a more personal and introspective approach to dance, contemporary offers a platform for exploration and self-discovery.

Jazz dance, with its roots in African American culture, is known for its energetic and dynamic movements. It combines elements of ballet, tap, and social dance, characterized by syncopated rhythms, isolations, and expressive gestures. Jazz dance is often associated with musical theater and popular entertainment, with a focus on showmanship and performance. It encourages dancers to embrace their personality and flair, making it a lively and engaging style for beginners. Jazz dance classes often incorporate upbeat music and choreography, providing a fun and vibrant atmosphere for learning.

Hip-hop dance, born from the streets of New York City in the 1970s, is a cultural movement that encompasses a variety of styles, including breaking, popping, and locking. It is characterized by its rhythmic and athletic movements, often performed to hip-hop music. Hip-hop dance emphasizes creativity, individuality, and self-expression, with an emphasis on freestyle and improvisation. It is a social and community-oriented style, often performed in battles or cyphers. For beginners, hip-hop offers an opportunity to connect with a vibrant and diverse culture, while developing rhythm, coordination, and confidence.

Tap dance, with its origins in African American and Irish dance traditions, is a percussive style that uses the sound of the dancer's shoes striking the floor as a form of rhythm and music. Tap dance is characterized by its intricate footwork, syncopated rhythms, and improvisational elements. It requires a keen sense of timing and musicality, as dancers create complex patterns and sounds with their feet. Tap dance classes often focus on developing rhythm, coordination, and precision, making it a challenging yet rewarding style for beginners.

Ballroom dance, a social and partner-based style, encompasses a variety of dances, including the waltz, tango, foxtrot, and cha-cha. It is characterized by its elegance, poise, and connection between partners.

Ballroom dance emphasizes posture, frame, and lead-and-follow techniques, requiring dancers to work in harmony with their partner. It is often performed in social settings, competitions, and showcases, offering a sense of community and camaraderie. For beginners, ballroom dance provides an opportunity to develop social skills, confidence, and grace.

Cultural and folk dances from around the world offer a glimpse into the traditions and heritage of different communities. These dances often reflect the history, values, and customs of a particular culture, providing a rich and diverse array of styles to explore. Examples include flamenco from Spain, bharatanatyam from India, and hula from Hawaii. Each of these styles carries its own unique movements, rhythms, and expressions, offering dancers an opportunity to connect with different cultures and broaden their understanding of the world.

Exploring different dance styles can enhance a dancer's versatility and adaptability, allowing them to draw inspiration from a wide range of influences. It encourages an open-minded and curious approach to learning, fostering creativity and innovation. By stepping outside of their comfort zone and embracing new challenges, dancers can discover new strengths and talents, enriching their overall dance experience.

For beginners, the journey of exploring different dance styles is an opportunity to discover their own unique voice and identity as a dancer. It allows them to experiment with different movements, rhythms, and expressions, finding the styles that resonate with them on a personal level. This exploration can lead to a deeper understanding of the art form and a greater appreciation for its diversity and richness.

Essential Footwork and Patterns

Footwork is the heartbeat of dance, the intricate tapestry of steps and patterns that form the foundation of movement. It is through footwork that dancers convey rhythm, style, and emotion, transforming music into a visual and kinetic experience. For beginners, mastering essential footwork and patterns is crucial, as it lays the groundwork for more complex choreography and enhances overall performance. Understanding the nuances of footwork requires attention to detail, practice, and a keen sense of timing and coordination.

At the core of effective footwork is the ability to maintain proper posture and alignment. This involves standing tall with the spine elongated, shoulders relaxed, and weight evenly distributed across both feet. Proper alignment ensures stability and balance, allowing dancers to execute footwork with precision and control. It also reduces the risk of injury, as it minimizes strain on the joints and muscles. Beginners should focus on developing a strong sense of body awareness, paying attention to how their posture and alignment affect their movement.

One of the most fundamental aspects of footwork is understanding weight transfer. This involves shifting the body's weight from one foot to the other, allowing for smooth and fluid transitions between steps. Weight transfer is essential for maintaining balance and momentum, and it plays a key role in executing turns, jumps, and directional changes. To practice weight transfer, dancers can start with simple exercises such as walking or marching in place, focusing on the sensation of shifting weight from heel to toe and from one foot to the other.

In addition to weight transfer, mastering basic foot positions is essential for executing footwork with accuracy and style. In many dance styles, there are specific foot positions that serve as the starting and ending points for various steps and patterns. For example, in ballet, the five basic positions of the feet provide a framework for movement, while in ballroom dance, the closed and open positions are fundamental to partner work. Beginners should familiarize themselves with the foot positions relevant to their chosen dance style, practicing them regularly to build muscle memory and confidence.

Patterns, or sequences of steps, are the building blocks of choreography. They provide structure and rhythm to a dance, allowing dancers to express musicality and creativity. Patterns can range from simple combinations of steps to complex sequences that require coordination and precision. For beginners, learning basic patterns is an important step in developing a strong dance foundation. These patterns often include common steps such as the grapevine, box step, or chasse, which can be adapted and incorporated into a variety of dance styles.

To effectively learn and execute patterns, dancers should focus on breaking them down into smaller, manageable components. This involves identifying the individual steps that make up the pattern and practicing them in isolation before combining them into a sequence. Repetition is key to building muscle memory and ensuring that the pattern becomes second nature. Dancers should also pay attention to the timing and rhythm of the pattern, practicing with music to develop a sense of musicality and synchronization.

Footwork is not only about the steps themselves but also about the quality and style of movement. This includes the use of dynamics, such as varying the speed, force, and intensity of steps to create contrast and expression. For example, a dancer might execute a series of quick, sharp steps followed by a slow, fluid movement to convey a change in mood or emotion. Experimenting with dynamics allows dancers to add depth and dimension to their footwork, enhancing their overall performance.

In addition to dynamics, the use of space is an important consideration in footwork. This involves understanding how to navigate the dance floor, using different directions, levels, and pathways to create visual interest and variety. Dancers should practice moving in different directions, such as forward, backward, sideways, and diagonally, as well as exploring different levels, such as high, medium, and low. This spatial awareness allows dancers to adapt their footwork to different settings and contexts, whether performing on stage or in a social dance setting.

For beginners, practicing footwork and patterns requires dedication and consistency. Regular practice helps reinforce muscle memory and build the strength and flexibility needed for dance. It's important to approach practice with patience and a positive attitude, recognizing that progress may be gradual and that mistakes are a natural part of the learning process. Setting realistic goals and tracking progress can provide motivation and a sense of accomplishment, encouraging dancers to continue their journey of exploration and growth.

Perfecting Arm and Hand Movements

Arm and hand movements are the silent storytellers of dance, weaving narratives and emotions into the fabric of performance. They add elegance, expressiveness, and nuance to a dancer's repertoire, transforming simple steps into a captivating visual symphony. For beginners, mastering the art of arm and hand movements is essential, as it enhances the overall aesthetic and emotional impact of their dance. Understanding the intricacies of these movements requires attention to detail, practice, and a deep connection to the music and narrative.

The foundation of effective arm and hand movements lies in understanding the role they play in dance. Arms and hands are not merely appendages; they are integral to the dancer's expression and communication. They can convey a wide range of emotions, from joy and excitement to sorrow and introspection. By mastering the language of arm and hand movements, dancers can create a more immersive and engaging experience for their audience.

One of the key elements of arm and hand movements is posture and alignment. Proper posture involves maintaining an upright and elongated spine, with the shoulders relaxed and the chest open. This alignment provides a stable base for the arms to move freely and expressively. Beginners should focus on developing a strong sense of body awareness, paying attention to how their posture and alignment affect their arm movements. Practicing in front of a mirror can be helpful, allowing dancers to observe and refine their technique.

In addition to posture, the quality of movement is crucial for effective arm and hand expressions. This includes the use of dynamics, such as varying the speed, force, and intensity of movements to create contrast and expression. For example, a dancer might execute a series of quick, sharp arm movements followed by a slow, fluid gesture to convey a change in mood or emotion. Experimenting with dynamics allows dancers to add depth and dimension to their performance, enhancing their overall expressiveness.

The use of space is another important consideration in arm and hand movements. This involves understanding how to navigate the space around the body, using different directions, levels, and pathways to create visual interest and variety. Dancers should practice moving their arms in different directions, such as forward, backward, sideways, and diagonally, as well as exploring different levels, such as high, medium, and low. This spatial awareness allows dancers to adapt their movements to different settings and contexts, whether performing on stage or in a social dance setting.

Incorporating gestures and motifs into arm and hand movements can also enhance a dancer's expressiveness. Gestures are symbolic movements that convey meaning or emotion, such as a wave, a point, or a reach. Motifs are recurring patterns or themes that add coherence and structure to a dance. By incorporating gestures and motifs into their movements, dancers can create a more cohesive and meaningful performance, connecting with their audience on a deeper level.

To develop effective arm and hand movements, beginners should focus on regular practice and repetition. Consistent training helps reinforce muscle memory and build the strength and flexibility needed for dance. It's important to approach practice with patience and a positive attitude, recognizing that progress may be gradual and that mistakes are a natural part of the learning process. Setting realistic goals and tracking progress can provide motivation and a sense of accomplishment, encouraging dancers to continue their journey of exploration and growth.

In addition to practice, feedback from instructors and peers is invaluable for refining arm and hand movements. Constructive criticism provides insights into areas for improvement and helps dancers refine their technique. It's important to approach feedback with an open mind and a willingness to learn, using it as a tool for growth and development. Dancers should also seek opportunities to observe and learn from more experienced dancers, gaining inspiration and insights from their practice.

Cross-training, or engaging in activities outside of dance, can also support the development of arm and hand movements. Activities such as yoga, Pilates, or swimming can enhance flexibility, strength, and coordination, providing a well-rounded approach to fitness. Cross-training can also prevent overuse injuries and promote overall health and well-being.

The Art of Spins and Turns

Spins and turns are the dazzling elements of dance that captivate audiences and elevate performances to new heights. They embody the grace, precision, and athleticism that define the art form, transforming simple movements into breathtaking displays of skill and artistry. For beginners, mastering the art of spins and turns is both a challenge and an opportunity, offering a pathway to greater confidence and expression on the dance floor. Understanding the mechanics and techniques behind these movements is essential for achieving balance, control, and fluidity.

The foundation of successful spins and turns lies in proper posture and alignment. Maintaining an upright and elongated spine, with the shoulders relaxed and the core engaged, provides the stability needed for rotation. This alignment ensures that the body remains centered and balanced throughout the turn, reducing the risk of wobbling or falling. Beginners should focus on developing a strong sense of body awareness, paying attention to how their posture and alignment affect their ability to spin and turn.

Spotting is a crucial technique for executing spins and turns with precision and control. It involves focusing the eyes on a fixed point in the direction of the turn, allowing the head to lead the rotation while the body follows. As the turn progresses, the head quickly snaps back to the focal point, helping to maintain balance and orientation. Spotting not only prevents dizziness but also enhances the aesthetic quality of the turn, creating a sense of fluidity and grace. Beginners should practice spotting in front of a mirror, gradually increasing the speed and complexity of their turns as they become more comfortable with the technique.

In addition to spotting, weight distribution plays a key role in executing spins and turns. Proper weight distribution involves shifting the body's weight onto the supporting leg, allowing the free leg to assist in the rotation. This balance between the supporting and free leg is essential for maintaining stability and momentum throughout the turn. Beginners should practice shifting their weight from one leg to the other, focusing on the sensation of grounding through the supporting leg while allowing the free leg to move freely.

The use of arms is another important consideration in spins and turns. Arms can provide momentum and balance, helping to initiate and control the rotation. For example, in a pirouette, the arms are often brought into a rounded position in front of the body, creating a compact shape that facilitates rotation. In other turns, such as fouettés or chaînés, the arms may open and close to generate momentum and maintain balance. Beginners should experiment with different arm positions and movements, exploring how they affect the speed and quality of their turns.

Developing core strength and stability is essential for executing spins and turns with control and precision. The core muscles, including the abdominals, obliques, and lower back, provide the support needed to maintain alignment and balance during rotation. Strengthening these muscles through exercises such as planks, sit-ups, and leg lifts can enhance a dancer's ability to execute turns with confidence and ease. Additionally, practicing balance exercises, such as standing on one leg or using a balance board, can improve stability and coordination.

Timing and rhythm are also crucial components of successful spins and turns. Understanding the musical cues and timing of a turn allows dancers to synchronize their movements with the music, creating a harmonious and expressive performance. Beginners should practice turning to different types of music, paying attention to the tempo, dynamics, and phrasing. This practice helps develop an intuitive sense of timing and rhythm, allowing dancers to execute turns with precision and musicality.

To master spins and turns, regular practice and repetition are essential. Consistent training helps reinforce muscle memory and build the strength and flexibility needed for dance. It's important to approach practice with patience and a positive attitude, recognizing that progress may be gradual and that mistakes are a natural part of the learning process. Setting realistic goals and tracking progress can provide motivation and a sense of accomplishment, encouraging dancers to continue their journey of exploration and growth.

Feedback from instructors and peers is invaluable for refining spins and turns. Constructive criticism provides insights into areas for improvement and helps dancers refine their technique. It's important to approach feedback with an open mind and a willingness to learn, using it as a tool for growth and development. Dancers should also seek opportunities to observe and learn from more experienced dancers, gaining inspiration and insights from their practice.

Cross-training, or engaging in activities outside of dance, can also support the development of spins and turns. Activities such as yoga, Pilates, or swimming can enhance flexibility, strength, and coordination, providing a well-rounded approach to fitness. Cross-training can also prevent overuse injuries and promote overall health and well-being.

Enhancing Your Dance Vocabulary

Dance is a language of movement, a form of expression that transcends words and communicates emotions, stories, and ideas. Just as a writer uses a rich vocabulary to craft compelling narratives, a dancer employs a diverse range of movements to convey meaning and artistry. Enhancing your dance vocabulary is an essential step in becoming a versatile and expressive dancer, allowing you to explore new styles, techniques, and creative possibilities. This journey involves expanding your repertoire of movements, refining your technique, and cultivating a deeper understanding of the art form.

The first step in enhancing your dance vocabulary is to immerse yourself in a variety of dance styles. Each style offers its own unique set of movements, rhythms, and expressions, providing a wealth of inspiration and knowledge. By exploring different styles, such as ballet, contemporary, jazz, hip-hop, and cultural dances, you can broaden your understanding of movement and discover new ways to express yourself. This exploration encourages an open-minded and curious approach to learning, fostering creativity and innovation.

As you delve into different dance styles, pay attention to the specific techniques and movements that define each one. For example, ballet emphasizes precision and grace, with movements such as pliés, tendus, and pirouettes forming the foundation of the style. Contemporary dance, on the other hand, often incorporates fluidity and improvisation, with an emphasis on floor work and abstract expression. By studying the techniques and movements of each style, you can build a diverse and versatile dance vocabulary that allows you to adapt to different contexts and challenges.

In addition to exploring different styles, refining your technique is crucial for enhancing your dance vocabulary. This involves developing a strong foundation in the fundamentals of dance, such as posture, alignment, balance, and coordination. These elements provide the stability and control needed to execute movements with precision and confidence. Regular practice and repetition are essential for reinforcing muscle memory and building the strength and flexibility needed for dance. As you refine your technique, focus on the quality and dynamics of your movements, experimenting with variations in speed, force, and intensity to add depth and dimension to your performance.

Improvisation is another valuable tool for expanding your dance vocabulary. It encourages spontaneity and creativity, allowing you to explore new movements and expressions without the constraints of choreography. Improvisation can be practiced individually or in groups, with or without music, and can involve a wide range of prompts and exercises. For example, you might explore different ways of moving through space, experiment with contrasting dynamics, or respond to a specific emotion or theme. By embracing improvisation, you can discover new possibilities for movement and expression, enhancing your overall dance vocabulary.

Incorporating gestures and motifs into your dance vocabulary can also enrich your performance. Gestures are symbolic movements that convey meaning or emotion, such as a wave, a point, or a reach. Motifs are recurring patterns or themes that add coherence and structure to a dance. By incorporating gestures and motifs into your movements, you can create a more cohesive and meaningful performance, connecting with your audience on a deeper level. Experiment with different gestures and motifs, exploring how they can be adapted and transformed to suit different styles and contexts.

To further enhance your dance vocabulary, seek inspiration from other art forms and disciplines. Music, visual art, theater, and literature can all provide valuable insights and ideas for movement and expression. For example, you might draw inspiration from the rhythm and dynamics of a piece of music, the imagery and symbolism of a painting, or the narrative and themes of a play or novel. By engaging with other art forms, you can expand your creative horizons and discover new ways to enrich your dance vocabulary.

Feedback from instructors and peers is invaluable for refining and expanding your dance vocabulary. Constructive criticism provides insights into areas for improvement and helps you refine your technique and expression. Approach feedback with an open mind and a willingness to learn, using it as a tool for growth and development. Additionally, seek opportunities to observe and learn from more experienced dancers, gaining inspiration and insights from their practice.

Cross-training, or engaging in activities outside of dance, can also support the development of your dance vocabulary. Activities such as yoga, Pilates, or martial arts can enhance flexibility, strength, and coordination, providing a well-rounded approach to fitness. Cross-training can also prevent overuse injuries and promote overall health and well-being, ensuring that your body is prepared for the demands of dance.

Chapter 4

Expressing Emotion Through Dance

The Role of Emotion in Dance

Emotion is the lifeblood of dance, infusing movement with depth, meaning, and resonance. It is the invisible thread that connects the dancer to the audience, transforming a series of steps into a powerful narrative that speaks to the heart. For beginners, understanding and harnessing the role of emotion in dance is a vital aspect of their artistic journey, offering a pathway to authenticity and expression. By exploring the interplay between emotion and movement, dancers can unlock new dimensions of creativity and connection.

At its core, dance is a form of storytelling, a way to convey experiences, ideas, and emotions without the need for words. Each movement, gesture, and expression carries a unique emotional weight, allowing dancers to communicate complex and nuanced narratives. Whether it's the joy of a celebratory dance, the sorrow of a poignant solo, or the tension of a dramatic pas de deux, emotion is the driving force that shapes the dancer's interpretation and performance.

To effectively convey emotion through dance, it is essential to cultivate a deep connection to the music and narrative. Music serves as the emotional backdrop for dance, providing the rhythm, dynamics, and mood that guide the dancer's expression. By immersing themselves in the music, dancers can tap into the emotional undercurrents that inform their movements, allowing them to convey a more authentic and compelling performance. This connection to the music is not just about following the beat; it's about feeling the music in every fiber of the body and allowing it to shape the dance.

In addition to music, the narrative or theme of a dance provides a framework for emotional expression. Whether it's a classical ballet with a well-defined storyline or a contemporary piece exploring abstract concepts, the narrative serves as a guide for the dancer's emotional journey. By understanding the context and themes of the dance, dancers can make informed choices about their movements and expressions, ensuring that their performance aligns with the intended message and impact.

One of the key elements of conveying emotion in dance is the use of facial expressions and body language. The face is a powerful tool for communication, capable of expressing a wide range of emotions, from joy and excitement to sadness and introspection. By using facial expressions in conjunction with movement, dancers can enhance the emotional impact of their performance, creating a more immersive and engaging experience for the audience. Similarly, body language, such as posture, gestures, and dynamics, plays a crucial role in conveying emotion, allowing dancers to express subtle nuances and shifts in mood.

To develop the ability to convey emotion through dance, beginners should focus on cultivating self-awareness and emotional intelligence. This involves exploring their own emotions and experiences, understanding how they manifest in the body, and learning to express them through movement. Improvisation is a valuable tool for this exploration, encouraging dancers to experiment with different emotions and expressions in a spontaneous and unstructured way. By embracing improvisation, dancers can discover new possibilities for emotional expression, enhancing their overall performance.

Feedback from instructors and peers is invaluable for refining emotional expression in dance. Constructive criticism provides insights into areas for improvement and helps dancers refine their technique and expression. It's important to approach feedback with an open mind and a willingness to learn, using it as a tool for growth and development. Additionally, observing and learning from more experienced dancers can provide inspiration and insights into the art of emotional expression.

Cross-training, or engaging in activities outside of dance, can also support the development of emotional expression. Activities such as acting, music, or visual art can enhance creativity, empathy, and emotional intelligence, providing a well-rounded approach to artistic development. Cross-training can also prevent burnout and promote overall well-being, ensuring that dancers are emotionally and physically prepared for the demands of dance.

Techniques for Emotional Expression

Emotional expression in dance is an art that transcends technical prowess, inviting dancers to delve into the depths of their own experiences and convey them through movement. It is the bridge between the dancer and the audience, transforming a performance into a shared emotional journey. For beginners, mastering techniques for emotional expression is a vital step in developing a unique and compelling dance style. This chapter explores various methods and practices that can help dancers tap into their emotions and translate them into powerful performances.

One of the most effective techniques for emotional expression is the use of improvisation. Improvisation encourages dancers to explore their emotions in a spontaneous and unstructured way, allowing them to discover new movements and expressions that resonate with their feelings. By setting aside choreography and embracing the freedom of improvisation, dancers can connect with their emotions on a deeper level, uncovering authentic expressions that might not emerge in a more structured setting. To practice improvisation, dancers can experiment with different prompts, such as responding to a piece of music, exploring a specific emotion, or imagining a narrative or scenario.

Visualization is another powerful tool for enhancing emotional expression. This technique involves creating vivid mental images or scenarios that evoke specific emotions, allowing dancers to embody those feelings in their movements. For example, a dancer might visualize a serene landscape to convey calmness or imagine a personal triumph to express joy and confidence. By engaging the imagination, dancers can access a rich tapestry of emotions and experiences, infusing their performances with depth and authenticity. Visualization can be practiced both in and out of the studio, providing a valuable resource for emotional exploration and expression.

Breath control is an often-overlooked aspect of emotional expression in dance. The breath is intimately connected to emotion, influencing the body's tension, relaxation, and overall energy. By becoming aware of their breath and learning to control it, dancers can enhance their emotional expression, using breath to convey subtle shifts in mood and intensity. For example, a deep, slow breath can evoke a sense of calm and introspection, while a quick, shallow breath can convey excitement or urgency. Practicing breath control through exercises such as yoga or meditation can help dancers develop greater awareness and mastery of this powerful tool.

Facial expressions and body language are essential components of emotional expression in dance. The face is a highly expressive tool, capable of conveying a wide range of emotions with subtlety and nuance. By using facial expressions in conjunction with movement, dancers can enhance the emotional impact of their performance, creating a more immersive and engaging experience for the audience. Similarly, body language, such as posture, gestures, and dynamics, plays a crucial role in conveying emotion, allowing dancers to express subtle nuances and shifts in mood. Practicing in front of a mirror or recording performances can help dancers refine their facial expressions and body language, ensuring that they align with the intended emotional message.

Music is a powerful catalyst for emotional expression, providing the rhythm, dynamics, and mood that guide the dancer's interpretation. By immersing themselves in the music, dancers can tap into the emotional undercurrents that inform their movements, allowing them to convey a more authentic and compelling performance. This connection to the music is not just about following the beat; it's about feeling the music in every fiber of the body and allowing it to shape the dance. Dancers should experiment with different genres and styles of music, exploring how each one influences their emotional expression and movement.

Feedback from instructors and peers is invaluable for refining emotional expression in dance. Constructive criticism provides insights into areas for improvement and helps dancers refine their technique and expression. It's important to approach feedback with an open mind and a willingness to learn, using it as a tool for growth and development. Additionally, observing and learning from more experienced dancers can provide inspiration and insights into the art of emotional expression.

Cross-training, or engaging in activities outside of dance, can also support the development of emotional expression. Activities such as acting, music, or visual art can enhance creativity, empathy, and emotional intelligence, providing a well-rounded approach to artistic development. Cross-training can also prevent burnout and promote overall well-being, ensuring that dancers are emotionally and physically prepared for the demands of dance.

Connecting with Your Audience

Connecting with an audience is the heart of any performance, transforming dance from a solitary act into a shared experience. It is the invisible bond that forms between the dancer and the viewer, a silent dialogue that transcends the boundaries of language and culture. For beginners, learning to connect with an audience is an essential skill that enhances the impact and authenticity of their performance. This chapter delves into the techniques and mindset needed to forge this connection, offering practical advice for dancers eager to captivate and engage their audience.

The first step in connecting with an audience is understanding the power of presence. Presence is the quality that draws the audience's attention and holds it, a magnetic force that makes a performance unforgettable. It is not about being the loudest or most flamboyant dancer on stage; rather, it is about being fully present in the moment, embodying the music and the movement with authenticity and conviction. To cultivate presence, dancers should focus on mindfulness and self-awareness, grounding themselves in the here and now and allowing their genuine emotions to shine through.

Eye contact is a powerful tool for establishing a connection with the audience. It creates a sense of intimacy and engagement, inviting viewers into the dancer's world and making them feel seen and acknowledged. By making eye contact with different members of the audience, dancers can create a personal connection that enhances the emotional impact of their performance. This technique requires confidence and vulnerability, as it involves opening oneself up to the gaze of others and sharing a piece of one's inner world.

Body language and facial expressions are also crucial components of audience connection. The way a dancer carries themselves, the gestures they use, and the expressions they wear all convey meaning and emotion, shaping the audience's perception of the performance. By using body language and facial expressions intentionally, dancers can enhance their storytelling and create a more immersive experience for the audience. Practicing in front of a mirror or recording performances can help dancers refine these elements, ensuring that they align with the intended message and emotion.

Understanding the audience's perspective is another key aspect of connection. Each audience is unique, with its own set of expectations, experiences, and cultural backgrounds. By considering the audience's perspective, dancers can tailor their performance to resonate with the viewers, creating a more meaningful and impactful experience. This might involve adapting the style, tone, or content of the performance to suit the audience's preferences or finding ways to incorporate elements that are relevant and relatable to them.

Storytelling is a powerful way to connect with an audience, transforming dance into a narrative that engages the viewer's imagination and emotions. By crafting a compelling story through movement, dancers can draw the audience into their world, inviting them to experience the journey alongside them. This requires a deep understanding of the narrative and themes of the dance, as well as the ability to convey them through movement, expression, and dynamics. Dancers should experiment with different storytelling techniques, exploring how they can use movement to convey character, plot, and emotion.

Music is another vital element in audience connection, serving as the emotional backdrop for the performance. By immersing themselves in the music, dancers can tap into its emotional undercurrents and convey them through their movements, creating a more authentic and compelling performance. This connection to the music is not just about following the beat; it's about feeling the music in every fiber of the body and allowing it to shape the dance. Dancers should experiment with different genres and styles of music, exploring how each one influences their emotional expression and movement.

Feedback from instructors and peers is invaluable for refining audience connection. Constructive criticism provides insights into areas for improvement and helps dancers refine their technique and expression. It's important to approach feedback with an open mind and a willingness to learn, using it as a tool for growth and development. Additionally, observing and learning from more experienced dancers can provide inspiration and insights into the art of audience connection.

Cross-training, or engaging in activities outside of dance, can also support the development of audience connection. Activities such as acting, music, or public speaking can enhance communication skills, empathy, and emotional intelligence, providing a well-rounded approach to artistic development. Cross-training can also prevent burnout and promote overall well-being, ensuring that dancers are emotionally and physically prepared for the demands of performance.

Storytelling Through Movement

Storytelling through movement is an ancient art form, a way to convey narratives and emotions without uttering a single word. It is a dance of imagination and expression, where each gesture, step, and pause weaves a tapestry of meaning that resonates with the audience. For dancers, mastering the art of storytelling through movement is a journey into the heart of creativity, offering a powerful means to communicate and connect. This chapter delves into the techniques and principles that can help dancers transform movement into a compelling narrative, providing practical guidance for those eager to explore this expressive dimension of dance.

At the core of storytelling through movement is the ability to convey a narrative arc. Just as a written story has a beginning, middle, and end, a dance narrative unfolds through a sequence of movements that guide the audience on a journey. The beginning sets the stage, introducing the characters, setting, and mood. The middle develops the plot, building tension and exploring themes. The end brings resolution, offering closure and reflection. To create a cohesive narrative arc, dancers must consider the structure and flow of their movements, ensuring that each section transitions smoothly and logically into the next.

Characterization is a vital element of storytelling through movement, allowing dancers to embody the personas and emotions of the narrative. By adopting distinct physical and emotional traits, dancers can bring characters to life, making them relatable and engaging for the audience. This involves exploring the character's motivations, desires, and conflicts, and expressing them through movement, facial expressions, and dynamics. Dancers should experiment with different characterizations, exploring how variations in posture, gesture, and energy can convey different personalities and emotions.

The use of motifs and themes is another powerful storytelling tool. Motifs are recurring patterns or movements that symbolize key ideas or emotions, adding coherence and depth to the narrative. Themes are the overarching concepts or messages that the story seeks to convey. By incorporating motifs and themes into their movements, dancers can create a more layered and meaningful performance, inviting the audience to engage with the narrative on multiple levels. Dancers should explore how motifs and themes can be adapted and transformed throughout the performance, creating a dynamic and evolving narrative.

Music plays a crucial role in storytelling through movement, providing the emotional and rhythmic foundation for the narrative. By aligning their movements with the music, dancers can enhance the emotional impact of their performance, creating a more immersive and compelling experience for the audience. This involves not only following the beat but also interpreting the dynamics, phrasing, and mood of the music, allowing it to shape the dance. Dancers should experiment with different musical genres and styles, exploring how each one influences their storytelling and expression.

Improvisation is a valuable technique for discovering new possibilities for storytelling through movement. It encourages spontaneity and creativity, allowing dancers to explore different narratives and expressions without the constraints of choreography. By setting aside preconceived notions and embracing the freedom of improvisation, dancers can tap into their intuition and imagination, uncovering authentic and original stories. Improvisation can be practiced individually or in groups, with or without music, and can involve a wide range of prompts and exercises.

Collaboration is another powerful tool for storytelling through movement, offering opportunities for dancers to combine their unique perspectives and talents. By working together, dancers can create richer and more complex narratives, drawing on each other's strengths and insights. Collaboration can take many forms, from co-creating choreography to sharing ideas and feedback. It requires open communication, trust, and a willingness to explore new possibilities, fostering a sense of community and shared creativity.

Feedback from instructors and peers is invaluable for refining storytelling through movement. Constructive criticism provides insights into areas for improvement and helps dancers refine their technique and expression. It's important to approach feedback with an open mind and a willingness to learn, using it as a tool for growth and development. Additionally, observing and learning from more experienced dancers can provide inspiration and insights into the art of storytelling through movement.

Cross-training, or engaging in activities outside of dance, can also support the development of storytelling skills. Activities such as acting, writing, or visual art can enhance creativity, empathy, and narrative understanding, providing a well-rounded approach to artistic development. Cross-training can also prevent burnout and promote overall well-being, ensuring that dancers are emotionally and physically prepared for the demands of storytelling through movement.

Finding Your Emotional Authenticity

Emotional authenticity in dance is the essence of genuine expression, a quality that transforms a technically proficient performance into a deeply moving experience. It is the dancer's ability to convey true emotions, drawn from personal experiences and inner truths, that resonates with audiences and creates a lasting impact. For beginners, finding emotional authenticity is a journey of self-discovery and vulnerability, requiring introspection and courage. This chapter explores the pathways to uncovering and embracing one's emotional authenticity, offering practical guidance for dancers eager to infuse their performances with sincerity and depth.

The journey to emotional authenticity begins with self-awareness. Understanding one's own emotions, triggers, and responses is crucial for conveying genuine feelings through movement. This involves taking the time to reflect on personal experiences, identifying the emotions they evoke, and exploring how these emotions manifest physically. Journaling can be a valuable tool in this process, providing a space for dancers to articulate their thoughts and feelings, and to draw connections between their inner world and their physical expression.

Mindfulness practices, such as meditation or yoga, can also enhance self-awareness by fostering a deeper connection between the mind and body. These practices encourage dancers to be present in the moment, to observe their thoughts and emotions without judgment, and to cultivate a sense of inner calm and clarity. By integrating mindfulness into their daily routine, dancers can develop greater emotional intelligence and resilience, equipping them to navigate the complexities of emotional expression with authenticity and grace.

Vulnerability is a key component of emotional authenticity, requiring dancers to open themselves up to the risk of being seen and judged. It involves embracing imperfections and uncertainties, and allowing oneself to be fully present and exposed in the moment. This can be a daunting prospect, particularly for beginners who may feel pressure to conform to external expectations or standards. However, vulnerability is also a source of strength and creativity, offering a pathway to deeper connection and expression. By embracing vulnerability, dancers can access a wellspring of authentic emotion, transforming their performances into powerful and resonant experiences.

Improvisation is a valuable technique for exploring emotional authenticity, encouraging dancers to experiment with different emotions and expressions in a spontaneous and unstructured way. By setting aside choreography and embracing the freedom of improvisation, dancers can tap into their intuition and imagination, uncovering authentic expressions that might not emerge in a more structured setting. Improvisation can be practiced individually or in groups, with or without music, and can involve a wide range of prompts and exercises. For example, dancers might explore different ways of moving through space, experiment with contrasting dynamics, or respond to a specific emotion or theme.

Feedback from instructors and peers is invaluable for refining emotional authenticity. Constructive criticism provides insights into areas for improvement and helps dancers refine their technique and expression. It's important to approach feedback with an open mind and a willingness to learn, using it as a tool for growth and development. Additionally, observing and learning from more experienced dancers can provide inspiration and insights into the art of emotional authenticity.

Music is a powerful catalyst for emotional authenticity, providing the rhythm, dynamics, and mood that guide the dancer's expression. By immersing themselves in the music, dancers can tap into the emotional undercurrents that inform their movements, allowing them to convey a more authentic and compelling performance. This connection to the music is not just about following the beat; it's about feeling the music in every fiber of the body and allowing it to shape the dance. Dancers should experiment with different genres and styles of music, exploring how each one influences their emotional expression and movement.

Cross-training, or engaging in activities outside of dance, can also support the development of emotional authenticity. Activities such as acting, music, or visual art can enhance creativity, empathy, and emotional intelligence, providing a well-rounded approach to artistic development. Cross-training can also prevent burnout and promote overall well-being, ensuring that dancers are emotionally and physically prepared for the demands of dance.

Chapter 5

Choreography and Creativity

The Basics of Choreography

Choreography is the art of crafting movement into a cohesive and expressive form, a dance that tells a story, conveys emotion, or explores abstract concepts. For beginners, understanding the basics of choreography is an essential step in developing their creative voice and artistic vision. This chapter delves into the foundational elements of choreography, offering practical guidance for those eager to embark on the journey of creating their own dance pieces.

At the heart of choreography is the concept of movement vocabulary. Just as a writer uses words to construct sentences and paragraphs, a choreographer uses movements to build phrases and sequences. Developing a rich and varied movement vocabulary is crucial for creating dynamic and engaging choreography. This involves exploring different styles and techniques, experimenting with a range of movements, and drawing inspiration from diverse sources. Dancers should immerse themselves in various dance forms, from classical ballet to contemporary, hip-hop to folk, to expand their repertoire and discover new possibilities for expression.

The structure of a dance piece is another fundamental aspect of choreography. A well-structured piece has a clear beginning, middle, and end, guiding the audience through a narrative or thematic journey. The beginning sets the stage, introducing the mood, characters, or themes. The middle develops the content, building tension, exploring ideas, or showcasing technical skills. The end brings resolution, offering closure or leaving the audience with a thought-provoking question. To create a cohesive structure, choreographers must consider the flow and pacing of their piece, ensuring that each section transitions smoothly and logically into the next.

Musicality is a key element of choreography, influencing the rhythm, dynamics, and mood of the dance. By aligning their movements with the music, choreographers can enhance the emotional impact of their piece, creating a more immersive and compelling experience for the audience. This involves not only following the beat but also interpreting the dynamics, phrasing, and mood of the music, allowing it to shape the dance. Choreographers should experiment with different musical genres and styles, exploring how each one influences their creative process and expression.

Spatial awareness is another important consideration in choreography. The use of space can convey meaning, create visual interest, and enhance the overall impact of the dance. Choreographers must think about how dancers move through space, the patterns they create, and the relationships between them. This involves exploring different formations, levels, and directions, as well as considering the use of props, sets, or lighting to enhance the spatial dynamics of the piece. By experimenting with spatial elements, choreographers can create a more engaging and visually striking performance.

Improvisation is a valuable tool for discovering new possibilities in choreography. It encourages spontaneity and creativity, allowing choreographers to explore different movements and expressions without the constraints of pre-planned sequences. By setting aside preconceived notions and embracing the freedom of improvisation, choreographers can tap into their intuition and imagination, uncovering authentic and original ideas. Improvisation can be practiced individually or in groups, with or without music, and can involve a wide range of prompts and exercises.

Collaboration is another powerful tool for choreography, offering opportunities for dancers to combine their unique perspectives and talents. By working together, choreographers and dancers can create richer and more complex pieces, drawing on each other's strengths and insights. Collaboration can take many forms, from co-creating choreography to sharing ideas and feedback. It requires open communication, trust, and a willingness to explore new possibilities, fostering a sense of community and shared creativity.

Feedback from instructors and peers is invaluable for refining choreography. Constructive criticism provides insights into areas for improvement and helps choreographers refine their technique and expression. It's important to approach feedback with an open mind and a willingness to learn, using it as a tool for growth and development. Additionally, observing and learning from more experienced choreographers can provide inspiration and insights into the art of choreography.

Cross-training, or engaging in activities outside of dance, can also support the development of choreographic skills. Activities such as acting, music, or visual art can enhance creativity, empathy, and narrative understanding, providing a well-rounded approach to artistic development. Cross-training can also prevent burnout and promote overall well-being, ensuring that choreographers are emotionally and physically prepared for the demands of creating dance.

Developing Your Creative Voice

Developing a creative voice in dance is akin to discovering a unique fingerprint—it's an expression of individuality, a reflection of personal experiences, and a manifestation of one's artistic vision. For beginners, this journey is both exhilarating and challenging, as it involves exploring uncharted territories of creativity and self-expression. This chapter delves into the process of cultivating a creative voice, offering practical insights and techniques to help dancers uncover and nurture their distinct artistic identity.

The first step in developing a creative voice is embracing curiosity. Curiosity fuels exploration and experimentation, encouraging dancers to step outside their comfort zones and discover new possibilities. It involves asking questions, seeking inspiration from diverse sources, and being open to new ideas and experiences. Dancers should immerse themselves in a wide range of dance styles, from classical to contemporary, hip-hop to folk, to broaden their horizons and expand their movement vocabulary. By exploring different genres and techniques, dancers can gather a rich tapestry of influences that inform and inspire their creative voice.

Self-reflection is another crucial aspect of this journey. Understanding one's own values, beliefs, and experiences is essential for authentic expression. This involves taking the time to reflect on personal stories, emotions, and aspirations, and considering how they can be translated into movement. Journaling can be a valuable tool in this process, providing a space for dancers to articulate their thoughts and feelings, and to draw connections between their inner world and their artistic expression. By engaging in self-reflection, dancers can gain clarity and insight into their unique perspective and voice.

Improvisation is a powerful technique for discovering and honing a creative voice. It encourages spontaneity and intuition, allowing dancers to explore different movements and expressions without the constraints of choreography. By setting aside preconceived notions and embracing the freedom of improvisation, dancers can tap into their imagination and uncover authentic and original ideas. Improvisation can be practiced individually or in groups, with or without music, and can involve a wide range of prompts and exercises. For example, dancers might explore different ways of moving through space, experiment with contrasting dynamics, or respond to a specific emotion or theme.

Collaboration is another valuable tool for developing a creative voice. Working with others offers opportunities for dancers to combine their unique perspectives and talents, creating richer and more complex pieces. Collaboration can take many forms, from co-creating choreography to sharing ideas and feedback. It requires open communication, trust, and a willingness to explore new possibilities, fostering a sense of community and shared creativity. By collaborating with others, dancers can gain new insights and inspiration, expanding their creative horizons and refining their voice.

Feedback from instructors and peers is invaluable for refining a creative voice. Constructive criticism provides insights into areas for improvement and helps dancers refine their technique and expression. It's important to approach feedback with an open mind and a willingness to learn, using it as a tool for growth and development. Additionally, observing and learning from more experienced dancers can provide inspiration and insights into the art of creative expression.

Music is a powerful catalyst for creativity, providing the rhythm, dynamics, and mood that guide the dancer's expression. By immersing themselves in the music, dancers can tap into its emotional undercurrents and convey them through their movements, allowing them to convey a more authentic and compelling performance. This connection to the music is not just about following the beat; it's about feeling the music in every fiber of the body and allowing it to shape the dance. Dancers should experiment with different genres and styles of music, exploring how each one influences their creative process and expression.

Cross-training, or engaging in activities outside of dance, can also support the development of a creative voice. Activities such as acting, music, or visual art can enhance creativity, empathy, and narrative understanding, providing a well-rounded approach to artistic development. Cross-training can also prevent burnout and promote overall well-being, ensuring that dancers are emotionally and physically prepared for the demands of dance.

Collaborating with Other Dancers

Collaboration in dance is a dynamic interplay of creativity, communication, and shared vision. It is the process of bringing together diverse talents and perspectives to create something greater than the sum of its parts. For beginners, collaborating with other dancers offers a wealth of opportunities for growth, learning, and artistic exploration. This chapter delves into the art of collaboration, providing practical insights and techniques to help dancers navigate the complexities and rewards of working together.

At the heart of successful collaboration is effective communication. Clear and open communication is essential for understanding each other's ideas, intentions, and expectations. It involves active listening, expressing thoughts and feelings honestly, and being receptive to feedback and suggestions. Dancers should cultivate an environment of trust and respect, where everyone feels comfortable sharing their perspectives and contributing to the creative process. This requires patience, empathy, and a willingness to compromise, as collaboration often involves balancing different viewpoints and finding common ground.

Establishing a shared vision is another crucial aspect of collaboration. A shared vision provides a guiding framework for the creative process, aligning the efforts and energies of all participants towards a common goal. This involves discussing and defining the themes, concepts, and objectives of the project, and ensuring that everyone is on the same page. Dancers should take the time to explore each other's ideas and inspirations, seeking to understand the unique contributions that each person brings to the table. By fostering a sense of collective ownership and purpose, dancers can create a more cohesive and unified piece.

Flexibility and adaptability are key qualities for successful collaboration. The creative process is often unpredictable and fluid, requiring dancers to be open to change and willing to explore new directions. This involves letting go of rigid expectations and embracing the unexpected, allowing the collaboration to evolve organically. Dancers should be prepared to experiment with different ideas, techniques, and approaches, and to adjust their contributions as needed. By remaining flexible and adaptable, dancers can navigate the challenges and opportunities of collaboration with creativity and resilience.

Conflict resolution is an inevitable part of collaboration, as differing opinions and perspectives can sometimes lead to disagreements. Effective conflict resolution involves addressing issues constructively and finding solutions that satisfy all parties. This requires open communication, active listening, and a focus on finding common ground. Dancers should approach conflicts with a positive and solution-oriented mindset, seeking to understand the underlying concerns and working together to find mutually beneficial outcomes. By handling conflicts with grace and diplomacy, dancers can strengthen their collaboration and build stronger relationships.

Improvisation is a valuable tool for collaborative exploration, encouraging spontaneity and creativity in the group dynamic. It allows dancers to experiment with different movements and expressions without the constraints of pre-planned choreography, fostering a sense of play and discovery. Improvisation can be practiced in pairs or groups, with or without music, and can involve a wide range of prompts and exercises. For example, dancers might explore different ways of moving through space, experiment with contrasting dynamics, or respond to a specific emotion or theme. By embracing improvisation, dancers can tap into their collective imagination and uncover new possibilities for collaboration.

Feedback and reflection are essential components of the collaborative process, providing opportunities for growth and improvement. Constructive feedback allows dancers to refine their technique and expression, while reflection encourages self-awareness and learning. Dancers should approach feedback with an open mind and a willingness to learn, using it as a tool for growth and development. Additionally, taking the time to reflect on the collaborative experience can provide valuable insights into the dynamics and outcomes of the project, informing future collaborations.

Cross-disciplinary collaboration can also enrich the creative process, offering new perspectives and insights from other art forms. Working with artists from different disciplines, such as musicians, visual artists, or actors, can inspire new ideas and approaches, expanding the creative possibilities of the collaboration. This requires openness to different ways of thinking and working, as well as a willingness to explore new techniques and concepts. By embracing cross-disciplinary collaboration, dancers can create more innovative and multidimensional pieces.

Improvisation Techniques

Improvisation in dance is a liberating and transformative practice, a space where creativity flows freely and the unexpected becomes a source of inspiration. It is the art of spontaneous movement, where dancers respond to their instincts, emotions, and surroundings without the constraints of pre-planned choreography. For beginners, mastering improvisation techniques is an exciting journey into the heart of self-expression and artistic exploration. This chapter delves into the world of improvisation, offering practical guidance and techniques to help dancers unlock their creative potential and embrace the freedom of movement.

Improvisation begins with the willingness to let go of perfection and embrace the unknown. It requires dancers to step outside their comfort zones, to trust their instincts, and to be open to whatever emerges in the moment. This mindset of openness and curiosity is essential for improvisation, as it allows dancers to explore new possibilities and discover their unique voice. To cultivate this mindset, dancers should practice mindfulness and presence, focusing on the sensations and emotions that arise as they move. By being fully present in the moment, dancers can tap into their intuition and respond authentically to the music, space, and their own bodies.

One of the foundational techniques in improvisation is exploring movement prompts. Prompts are cues or ideas that inspire movement, providing a starting point for exploration. They can be based on a wide range of elements, such as emotions, images, words, or physical sensations. For example, a dancer might use the prompt "flow like water" to explore fluid and continuous movements, or "sharp and angular" to experiment with contrasting dynamics. By using prompts, dancers can break free from habitual patterns and discover new ways of moving, expanding their movement vocabulary and creative expression.

Another key technique is exploring different qualities of movement. Movement qualities refer to the characteristics or attributes of a movement, such as its speed, weight, or energy. By experimenting with different qualities, dancers can create a rich and varied palette of expression, adding depth and nuance to their improvisation. For example, a dancer might explore movements that are light and airy, heavy and grounded, or sharp and percussive. By playing with these qualities, dancers can convey a wide range of emotions and ideas, creating a more dynamic and engaging improvisation.

Improvisation also involves exploring the use of space. Space is a powerful element in dance, influencing the way movements are perceived and experienced. Dancers should experiment with different spatial patterns, levels, and directions, considering how they can enhance the overall impact of their improvisation. For example, a dancer might explore moving in a circular pattern, using different levels to create contrast, or moving in and out of the floor to add dimension. By being aware of the space around them, dancers can create more visually interesting and dynamic improvisations.

Music is a powerful catalyst for improvisation, providing the rhythm, dynamics, and mood that guide the dancer's expression. By immersing themselves in the music, dancers can tap into its emotional undercurrents and convey them through their movements. This connection to the music is not just about following the beat; it's about feeling the music in every fiber of the body and allowing it to shape the dance. Dancers should experiment with different genres and styles of music, exploring how each one influences their improvisation and expression.

Partner and group improvisation offer unique opportunities for exploration and connection. Working with others encourages dancers to respond to each other's movements, creating a dynamic interplay of energy and expression. This involves being attuned to the movements and intentions of others, and being open to the possibilities that arise from collaboration. Partner and group improvisation can involve a wide range of exercises, such as mirroring, leading and following, or creating a movement conversation. By engaging in partner and group improvisation, dancers can develop their ability to communicate and connect through movement, enhancing their overall improvisational skills.

Feedback and reflection are essential components of the improvisation process, providing opportunities for growth and improvement. Constructive feedback allows dancers to refine their technique and expression, while reflection encourages self-awareness and learning. Dancers should approach feedback with an open mind and a willingness to learn, using it as a tool for growth and development. Additionally, taking the time to reflect on their improvisation experiences can provide valuable insights into their creative process and expression, informing future improvisations.

Bringing Your Choreography to Life

Breathing life into choreography is an exhilarating process that transforms abstract ideas into tangible, emotive performances. It's the moment when a choreographer's vision takes shape, when movements crafted in the mind become a living, breathing dance. For beginners, this journey from concept to stage is both a creative challenge and an opportunity for profound artistic expression. This chapter delves into the essential steps and techniques for bringing choreography to life, offering practical guidance to help dancers and choreographers realize their artistic visions.

The journey begins with a clear and compelling concept. A strong concept serves as the foundation for the entire piece, providing direction and coherence. It could be a story, an emotion, a theme, or even an abstract idea. The key is to ensure that the concept resonates with the choreographer and has the potential to engage and move the audience. Once the concept is established, it's important to flesh out the details, considering how the movements, music, and staging will convey the intended message or emotion. This involves brainstorming and sketching out ideas, experimenting with different approaches, and refining the concept until it feels fully realized.

Selecting the right music is a crucial step in bringing choreography to life. Music sets the tone and mood of the piece, guiding the rhythm and dynamics of the movements. It's important to choose music that complements and enhances the concept, creating a harmonious relationship between sound and movement. Dancers should immerse themselves in the music, allowing it to inform and inspire their choreography. This involves listening deeply to the nuances of the music, feeling its emotional undercurrents, and considering how the movements can reflect and amplify these elements. Experimenting with different musical genres and styles can also open up new creative possibilities and add depth to the choreography.

Crafting the choreography itself is a process of exploration and refinement. It involves translating the concept into a series of movements and sequences that convey the intended message or emotion. This requires a deep understanding of movement vocabulary and technique, as well as a willingness to experiment and take risks. Choreographers should explore different movement qualities, dynamics, and spatial patterns, considering how each element contributes to the overall impact of the piece. It's important to remain open to new ideas and directions, allowing the choreography to evolve organically and authentically.

Rehearsals are where the choreography truly begins to come to life. They provide an opportunity to refine and polish the movements, ensuring that they are executed with precision and expression. Rehearsals also allow dancers to internalize the choreography, developing a deep connection to the movements and the music. This involves practicing consistently and diligently, paying attention to details such as timing, alignment, and expression. It's important to create a supportive and collaborative rehearsal environment, where dancers feel comfortable experimenting and offering feedback. Constructive criticism and open communication are essential for refining the choreography and ensuring that it aligns with the original concept.

Staging and production elements play a significant role in bringing choreography to life. Lighting, costumes, and sets can enhance the visual and emotional impact of the piece, creating a more immersive and engaging experience for the audience. Choreographers should consider how these elements can complement and amplify the choreography, adding depth and dimension to the performance. This involves collaborating with designers and technicians, discussing ideas and concepts, and experimenting with different options. It's important to ensure that the staging and production elements align with the overall vision and concept, creating a cohesive and unified performance.

Performance is the culmination of the choreographic process, the moment when the piece is shared with an audience. It's an opportunity for dancers to connect with the audience, to convey the emotions and ideas that inspired the choreography. This requires confidence, presence, and authenticity, as well as a deep connection to the movements and the music. Dancers should focus on conveying the essence of the piece, allowing their passion and expression to shine through. It's important to remain present and engaged, responding to the energy of the audience and the moment.

Feedback and reflection are valuable tools for growth and improvement. Constructive feedback from instructors, peers, and audience members can provide insights into areas for refinement and development. Dancers should approach feedback with an open mind and a willingness to learn, using it as a tool for growth and development. Reflection allows dancers to gain insights into their creative process and performance, informing future projects and collaborations. By taking the time to reflect on their experiences, dancers can deepen their understanding of their artistic voice and vision.

Chapter 6

Performance Preparation and Stage Presence

Preparing Mentally and Physically

Preparing for a dance performance is a holistic endeavor that requires both mental and physical readiness. The synergy between mind and body is crucial for delivering a compelling and seamless performance. For beginners, understanding how to prepare mentally and physically is essential for building confidence, enhancing performance quality, and ensuring overall well-being. This chapter delves into the strategies and techniques that dancers can employ to achieve optimal mental and physical preparation.

Mental preparation begins with cultivating a positive mindset. The way dancers perceive themselves and their abilities can significantly impact their performance. It's important to foster self-belief and confidence, acknowledging strengths while also recognizing areas for growth. Visualization is a powerful tool in this process. By mentally rehearsing the choreography, dancers can create a vivid image of their performance, imagining themselves executing each movement with precision and grace. This mental rehearsal helps to build familiarity and confidence, reducing anxiety and enhancing focus.

Setting clear and achievable goals is another key aspect of mental preparation. Goals provide direction and motivation, helping dancers to stay focused and committed to their practice. These goals should be specific, measurable, and realistic, allowing dancers to track their progress and celebrate their achievements. Whether it's mastering a particular technique, improving stamina, or enhancing expression, having clear goals can guide dancers in their preparation and keep them motivated throughout the process.

Mindfulness and relaxation techniques can also support mental preparation by reducing stress and promoting focus. Practices such as meditation, deep breathing, and yoga can help dancers to center themselves, calm their minds, and enhance their concentration. These techniques encourage dancers to be present in the moment, allowing them to connect more deeply with their movements and the music. By incorporating mindfulness and relaxation into their routine, dancers can cultivate a sense of calm and clarity, enhancing their overall mental readiness.

Physical preparation is equally important, as it ensures that the body is conditioned and ready for the demands of dance. A comprehensive warm-up routine is essential for preventing injuries and optimizing performance. This routine should include dynamic stretches, strength exercises, and cardiovascular activities that target the muscles and joints used in dance. By gradually increasing the intensity of the warm-up, dancers can prepare their bodies for the physical demands of the choreography, enhancing flexibility, strength, and endurance.

Cross-training is a valuable component of physical preparation, offering a well-rounded approach to fitness and conditioning. Engaging in activities such as swimming, Pilates, or strength training can complement dance practice by enhancing overall fitness, balance, and coordination. Cross-training can also prevent overuse injuries by targeting different muscle groups and promoting overall body awareness. By incorporating a variety of physical activities into their routine, dancers can build a strong and resilient body, ready to tackle the challenges of dance.

Nutrition and hydration play a crucial role in physical preparation, providing the energy and nutrients needed for optimal performance. A balanced diet rich in carbohydrates, proteins, and healthy fats supports muscle function and recovery, while adequate hydration ensures that the body remains energized and alert. Dancers should pay attention to their nutritional needs, fueling their bodies with wholesome foods and staying hydrated throughout the day. This involves planning meals and snacks that provide sustained energy, as well as drinking water regularly to maintain hydration levels.

Rest and recovery are essential components of both mental and physical preparation. Adequate rest allows the body to repair and regenerate, while also supporting mental clarity and focus. Dancers should prioritize sleep, aiming for seven to nine hours per night to ensure optimal recovery and performance. Additionally, incorporating rest days into their routine can prevent burnout and overtraining, allowing the body and mind to recharge and rejuvenate. By balancing practice with rest and recovery, dancers can maintain their energy and enthusiasm, enhancing their overall preparation.

Feedback and reflection are valuable tools for both mental and physical preparation, providing insights into areas for improvement and growth. Constructive feedback from instructors and peers can help dancers refine their technique and expression, while reflection encourages self-awareness and learning. Dancers should approach feedback with an open mind and a willingness to learn, using it as a tool for growth and development. Additionally, taking the time to reflect on their preparation process can provide valuable insights into their strengths and areas for improvement, informing future practice and performance.

Costume and Makeup Tips

Costume and makeup are integral elements of a dance performance, serving as visual extensions of the choreography and enhancing the overall storytelling. They have the power to transform dancers into characters, evoke specific moods, and create a cohesive aesthetic that captivates the audience. For beginners, understanding the nuances of costume and makeup design is essential for creating a polished and professional presentation. This chapter offers practical tips and insights to help dancers navigate the world of costume and makeup, ensuring that their visual presentation complements and elevates their performance.

The first step in costume design is understanding the concept and theme of the performance. Costumes should align with the narrative and emotional tone of the piece, enhancing the story being told through movement. Whether the dance is a classical ballet, a contemporary piece, or a cultural folk dance, the costume should reflect the essence of the choreography. This involves considering factors such as color, fabric, and style, and how they contribute to the overall aesthetic. For example, a flowing, ethereal costume might be appropriate for a lyrical piece, while bold, structured attire could suit a more dynamic and powerful performance.

Comfort and functionality are paramount when selecting costumes. Dancers need to move freely and confidently, without being restricted by their attire. It's important to choose fabrics that allow for ease of movement and breathability, such as stretchable materials that accommodate a range of motion. Additionally, costumes should be tailored to fit well, avoiding any loose or tight areas that could hinder performance. Practical considerations, such as secure fastenings and reinforced seams, are also essential to prevent wardrobe malfunctions during the performance.

Layering can be an effective technique in costume design, adding depth and versatility to the visual presentation. By incorporating different layers, dancers can create dynamic transformations throughout the performance, revealing new elements or changing the silhouette. This can be achieved through the use of removable skirts, jackets, or accessories that can be added or removed as the choreography progresses. Layering not only enhances the visual interest of the costume but also allows for creative storytelling through costume changes.

Makeup is another powerful tool for enhancing the visual impact of a performance. It serves to highlight facial expressions, define features, and create a cohesive look that complements the costume and choreography. When applying makeup, it's important to consider the lighting and distance from the audience, as these factors can affect how makeup appears on stage. Stage makeup typically requires more intensity and contrast than everyday makeup to ensure that features are visible from afar. This involves using bold colors, defined lines, and strategic highlighting and contouring to enhance the dancer's appearance.

The choice of makeup should also align with the character and theme of the performance. For example, a classical ballet might call for a more traditional and elegant makeup look, while a contemporary piece could allow for more creative and avant-garde styles. Dancers should experiment with different makeup techniques and products, considering how they can enhance the overall aesthetic and storytelling of the performance. It's important to practice applying makeup in advance, ensuring that the look is polished and consistent for each performance.

Hair styling is an extension of makeup and costume design, contributing to the overall visual presentation. The hairstyle should complement the costume and makeup, enhancing the character and theme of the performance. Practicality is key, as the hairstyle must be secure and comfortable, allowing the dancer to move freely without distraction. This involves using appropriate hair products and accessories, such as pins, elastics, and hairspray, to ensure that the hairstyle remains intact throughout the performance. Dancers should also consider how the hairstyle interacts with the costume, avoiding any elements that could become entangled or obstruct movement.

Accessories can add the finishing touch to a costume, providing additional detail and interest. Whether it's jewelry, hats, or props, accessories should be chosen carefully to enhance the overall aesthetic without overwhelming the costume. They should be securely attached and easy to manage, ensuring that they do not interfere with the dancer's movements. Accessories can also serve as storytelling elements, adding depth and context to the character or theme of the performance.

Rehearsing in costume and makeup is an essential step in the preparation process, allowing dancers to become accustomed to their attire and make any necessary adjustments. This involves practicing the choreography in full costume and makeup, considering how the elements interact with the movements and making any modifications as needed. Rehearsing in costume also provides an opportunity to address any practical concerns, such as costume changes, makeup touch-ups, or accessory management, ensuring a smooth and seamless performance.

Overcoming Stage Fright

Stage fright is a common experience for performers, a mix of excitement and anxiety that can manifest as a racing heart, shaky hands, or a mind that suddenly goes blank. For dancers, overcoming stage fright is a crucial step in delivering a confident and engaging performance. It involves understanding the roots of this fear, developing strategies to manage it, and transforming nervous energy into a powerful stage presence. This chapter offers practical advice and techniques to help dancers conquer stage fright and embrace the joy of performing.

Understanding the nature of stage fright is the first step in overcoming it. At its core, stage fright is a natural response to the pressure of performing in front of an audience. It's a combination of adrenaline and self-awareness, a heightened state that can either hinder or enhance performance.

Recognizing that stage fright is a common and normal experience can help dancers reframe their perspective, viewing it as a sign of their passion and commitment rather than a barrier to success.

Preparation is a powerful antidote to stage fright. The more prepared a dancer feels, the more confident they will be on stage. This involves thorough rehearsal, ensuring that the choreography is second nature and that every movement is ingrained in muscle memory. Practicing in different environments, such as in front of mirrors, peers, or even recording oneself, can help simulate the experience of performing for an audience. By becoming intimately familiar with the choreography, dancers can reduce the fear of forgetting steps and focus on expressing themselves fully.

Visualization is a technique that can help dancers mentally prepare for a performance. By imagining themselves on stage, executing each movement with precision and grace, dancers can create a mental blueprint of success. This involves visualizing not only the steps but also the emotions, expressions, and energy they wish to convey. Visualization can be practiced in a quiet space, allowing dancers to immerse themselves in the experience and build confidence in their abilities.

Breathing exercises are an effective way to manage the physical symptoms of stage fright. Deep, controlled breathing can help calm the nervous system, reducing anxiety and promoting relaxation. Techniques such as diaphragmatic breathing, where the focus is on expanding the abdomen rather than the chest, can be particularly beneficial. By practicing these exercises regularly, dancers can develop a sense of control over their physiological responses, allowing them to remain calm and focused on stage.

Positive self-talk is another valuable tool for overcoming stage fright. The way dancers speak to themselves can significantly impact their confidence and performance. Replacing negative thoughts with positive affirmations can help shift the mindset from fear to empowerment. Phrases such as "I am prepared," "I am capable," and "I am excited to share my dance" can reinforce self-belief and reduce anxiety. By cultivating a positive inner dialogue, dancers can build resilience and approach the stage with confidence.

Connecting with the audience is a powerful way to transform stage fright into a positive experience. Rather than viewing the audience as a source of judgment, dancers can see them as partners in the performance, sharing in the joy and emotion of the dance. Making eye contact, smiling, and engaging with the audience can create a sense of connection and support, reducing feelings of isolation and fear.

By focusing on the shared experience, dancers can shift their attention away from self-consciousness and towards the joy of performing.

Grounding techniques can help dancers stay present and focused during a performance. These techniques involve anchoring oneself in the present moment, using sensory awareness to maintain focus and calm. Simple actions such as feeling the floor beneath the feet, noticing the rhythm of the music, or focusing on the breath can help dancers remain centered and engaged. By practicing grounding techniques, dancers can enhance their stage presence and deliver a more authentic and expressive performance.

Support from peers and mentors can also play a crucial role in overcoming stage fright. Sharing experiences and receiving encouragement from others can provide reassurance and build confidence. Dancers should seek out supportive environments where they can express their fears and receive constructive feedback. Mentors and instructors can offer valuable insights and techniques for managing stage fright, drawing from their own experiences to guide and inspire.

Embracing the excitement of performing is a powerful way to reframe stage fright. Rather than viewing nervousness as a negative emotion, dancers can see it as a sign of their passion and dedication. The adrenaline that accompanies stage fright can be harnessed as a source of energy and intensity, enhancing the performance and adding depth to the expression. By embracing the excitement and channeling it into their dance, dancers can transform stage fright into a powerful and positive force.

Engaging with Your Audience

Engaging with an audience is an art form in itself, a dance that extends beyond the physical movements on stage. It is the invisible thread that connects performers to their viewers, transforming a dance into a shared experience. For beginners, mastering the skill of audience engagement is crucial for creating memorable and impactful performances. This chapter delves into the techniques and strategies that dancers can employ to captivate and connect with their audience, ensuring that their performance resonates long after the final bow.

The foundation of audience engagement lies in authenticity. Audiences are drawn to genuine expression, to the raw emotions and stories that unfold through movement. Dancers should strive to be true to themselves and their artistic vision, allowing their personality and passion to shine through. This authenticity creates a sense of trust and connection, inviting the audience to invest emotionally in the performance. By embracing their individuality and expressing their unique voice, dancers can create a powerful and compelling presence on stage.

Storytelling is a powerful tool for engaging an audience. Every dance tells a story, whether it's a narrative tale, an abstract exploration, or an emotional journey. Dancers should consider the story they wish to convey and how their movements, expressions, and energy can bring it to life. This involves crafting a clear and coherent narrative, using dynamics, timing, and spatial patterns to enhance the storytelling. By weaving a captivating story through their dance, performers can draw the audience into their world, creating a shared experience that resonates on a deeper level.

Eye contact is a simple yet effective way to connect with an audience. It creates a direct line of communication, breaking down the barrier between performer and viewer. By making eye contact, dancers can convey emotions, intentions, and energy, inviting the audience to engage with the performance on a personal level. This connection can be established with individual audience members or with the audience as a whole, creating a sense of intimacy and involvement. Eye contact should be used thoughtfully and intentionally, enhancing the overall impact of the performance.

Energy is a vital component of audience engagement. The energy that dancers bring to the stage is contagious, influencing the mood and atmosphere of the performance. Dancers should be mindful of their energy levels, ensuring that they are fully present and committed to each moment. This involves channeling their passion and enthusiasm into their movements, creating a vibrant and dynamic performance that captivates the audience. By maintaining a strong and consistent energy, dancers can sustain the audience's attention and create a memorable experience.

Body language is another key element of audience engagement. The way dancers carry themselves, their posture, and their gestures all contribute to the overall impression they create on stage. Confident and open body language can convey assurance and invite the audience to engage, while closed or hesitant movements may create a sense of distance.

Dancers should be aware of their body language, using it to reinforce the emotions and intentions of their performance. This involves being conscious of their alignment, facial expressions, and gestures, ensuring that they align with the overall narrative and mood.

Interaction with fellow performers can also enhance audience engagement. The chemistry and connection between dancers can create a dynamic and compelling performance, drawing the audience into the relationships and stories being portrayed. This involves being attuned to the movements and intentions of others, responding to their energy and creating a cohesive and harmonious performance. By fostering a sense of collaboration and connection on stage, dancers can create a more engaging and immersive experience for the audience.

Adaptability is an important skill for engaging with an audience. Every performance is unique, and dancers should be prepared to respond to the energy and reactions of the audience. This involves being flexible and open to change, adjusting their performance to suit the mood and atmosphere of the moment. Whether it's slowing down a movement to savor a poignant moment or amplifying the energy to match the audience's enthusiasm, adaptability allows dancers to create a more responsive and engaging performance.

Feedback from the audience can provide valuable insights into the effectiveness of engagement strategies. Observing the audience's reactions, such as applause, laughter, or silence, can offer clues about what resonates and what may need adjustment. Dancers should be open to feedback, using it as a tool for growth and improvement. This involves reflecting on their performance, considering what worked well and what could be enhanced, and incorporating these insights into future performances.

Evaluating Your Performance

Evaluating a performance is a crucial step in the journey of any dancer, offering a pathway to growth, refinement, and deeper artistic understanding. It is through thoughtful evaluation that dancers can identify strengths, recognize areas for improvement, and set goals for future development. For beginners, learning how to effectively evaluate their performances is an essential skill that fosters continuous learning and artistic evolution. This chapter provides practical guidance on how to approach performance evaluation, offering insights and techniques to help dancers reflect on their work with clarity and purpose.

The first step in evaluating a performance is to adopt a mindset of openness and curiosity. It's important to approach the evaluation process with a willingness to learn and grow, rather than a focus on criticism or judgment. This involves viewing the performance as a learning opportunity, a chance to gain insights into one's artistic journey and to celebrate achievements while acknowledging areas for improvement. By cultivating a positive and constructive mindset, dancers can create a supportive environment for self-reflection and growth.

Self-assessment is a valuable tool in the evaluation process, allowing dancers to reflect on their own experiences and perceptions of the performance. This involves considering various aspects of the performance, such as technical execution, emotional expression, and overall impact. Dancers should ask themselves questions such as: Did I convey the intended emotions and story? Was my technique clean and precise? How did I connect with the audience? By reflecting on these questions, dancers can gain a deeper understanding of their performance and identify specific areas for improvement.

Video recordings can be an invaluable resource for performance evaluation, providing an objective perspective on the dance. Watching a recording of the performance allows dancers to observe their movements, expressions, and interactions from the audience's point of view. This can reveal details that may have been overlooked during the performance, offering insights into timing, spacing, and dynamics. When reviewing a video, it's important to focus on both strengths and areas for growth, taking note of moments that were particularly effective and those that could be enhanced.

Feedback from instructors, peers, and mentors is another essential component of performance evaluation. Constructive feedback provides an external perspective, offering insights and suggestions that can inform future practice and development. Dancers should seek feedback from trusted sources who can provide honest and supportive critiques. It's important to approach feedback with an open mind, considering the insights offered and how they align with one's own self-assessment. By integrating feedback into their evaluation process, dancers can gain a more comprehensive understanding of their performance.

Setting specific and achievable goals is a key outcome of the evaluation process. Goals provide direction and motivation, guiding dancers in their practice and development. These goals should be informed by the insights gained from self-assessment, video review, and feedback, focusing on areas that will enhance overall performance quality. Whether it's improving a particular technique, enhancing emotional expression, or refining stage presence, setting clear goals can help dancers stay focused and committed to their artistic journey.

Reflection is an ongoing process that extends beyond the immediate evaluation of a performance. It involves considering how the insights gained from evaluation can inform future practice and development. Dancers should take the time to reflect on their progress, considering how their goals and priorities may evolve over time. This reflection can be supported by keeping a journal or log of performances, noting key insights, achievements, and areas for growth. By maintaining a record of their artistic journey, dancers can track their progress and celebrate their development over time.

Collaboration and discussion with fellow dancers can also enhance the evaluation process, offering opportunities for shared learning and growth. Engaging in conversations about performances, techniques, and artistic choices can provide new perspectives and insights. Dancers can learn from each other's experiences, sharing tips, strategies, and feedback that can inform their own practice. By fostering a sense of community and collaboration, dancers can create a supportive environment for evaluation and growth.